Patchwork Quilts
Made Easy

REVISED, 2ND EDITION

JEAN WELLS

33 QUILT FAVORITES, OLD & NEW

FOREWORD BY ALEX ANDERSON

C&T PUBLISHING

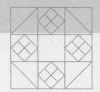

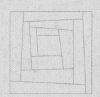

Dedication

To the thousands of students
that I have had the pleasure of
teaching throughout the years.
Creating quilters is my joy.

© 2003 Jean Wells
Editor-in-Chief: Darra Williamson
Editor: Candie Frankel
Technical Editors: Candie Frankel, Joyce Lytle
Copyeditor/Proofreader: Carol Barrett, Stacy Chamness
Cover Designer: Christina D. Jarumay
Design Director/Book Designer: Christina D. Jarumay
Illustrator: Jeffrey Carrillo
Production Assistant: Tim Manibusan
Photography: All styled quilt photos (except pages 66–67) and photos on pages 21 (flowers), 33, and 34 by Valori Wells. All photos of Jean Wells and quilt photos on pages 66–67, 74, 78, 99, 122, 140, and 146 by Ross Chandler. All flat quilt and block photos, except as noted above, by Sharon Risedorph. All other photos by C&T staff.
Published by C&T Publishing, Inc., P.O. Box 1456, Lafayette, California 94549

Front cover: *Fresh Produce* by Jean Wells; photographed by Valori Wells at Richard's Produce, Sisters, Oregon.
Back cover: *Springtime Meadow* by Jean Wells; photo by Valori Wells. Quilt block photos by Ross Chandler and Sharon Risedorph.

Attention Copy Shops: Please note the following exception—Publisher and author give permission to photocopy template patterns and quilting designs for personal use only.

Attention Teachers: C&T Publishing, Inc. encourages you to use this book as a text for teaching. Contact us at 800-284-1114 or www.ctpub.com for more information about the C&T Teachers Program.

We take great care to ensure that the information included in this book is accurate and presented in good faith, but no warranty is provided nor results guaranteed. Having no control over the choices of materials or procedures used, neither the author nor C&T Publishing, Inc. shall have any liability to any person or entity with respect to any loss or damage caused directly or indirectly by the information contained in this book. For your convenience, we post an up-to-date listing of corrections on our web page (www.ctpub.com). If a correction is not already noted, please contact our customer service department at ctinfo@ctpub.com or at PO Box 1456, Lafayette, California 94549.

Trademarked (™) and Registered Trademark (®) names are used throughout this book. Rather than use the symbols with every occurrence of a trademark and registered trademark name, we are using the names only in the editorial fashion and to the benefit of the owner, with no intention of infringement.

Library of Congress Cataloging-in-Publication Data
Wells, Jean.
  Patchwork quilts made easy : 33 quilt favorites, old & new / Jean Wells ; foreword by Alex Anderson.
    p. cm.
  ISBN 1-57120-196-3 (paper trade)
  1. Patchwork--Patterns. 2. Machine quilting--Patterns. I. Title.
  TT835 .W4654 2003
  746.46'041--dc21

2002151468

Printed in China
10 9 8 7 6 5 4 3 2 1

Acknowledgments

In the past twenty-three years I have written over twenty different how-to quilting books. Creating a book is an involved process, with many different people assisting in a variety of ways, from sewing to photography to laying out the pages.

I would first of all like to thank Margaret Peters, my very good friend, who encouraged me to revise and update *Patchwork Quilts Made Easy*. The first version was a huge success, thanks in part to the support of my longtime friend Ursula Searles. She continues to inspire me in all that I do.

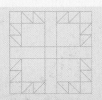

As I set into a three-month fury of creating and writing directions for twenty-seven new quilts, my dependable staff kept The Stitchin' Post humming. Their support in so many ways is overwhelming. A special thank-you to Lawry Thorn, Valori Wells, and Sally Brittain, who manage the happenings at the The Stitchin' Post on a day-to-day basis. Betsy Mennesson, my personal assistant, gracefully takes care of tasks, reminds me of commitments, helps me follow through, lends an ear when needed—and stitches beautifully.

Many talented quilters helped with the sewing. Barbara Ferguson, my own personal "sewing fairy," pieces and quilts with enthusiasm and is so good with color ideas and encouragement. Gerri Moore and Victoria Brady buttonhole-stitched appliqués and hand-stitched bindings. Carolyn Franks, June Jaeger, Angie McGuire, Sue McMahan, Joanne Myers, Nadine Partridge, Karen Shadley, and Laura Simmons helped by assembling the quilts and hand-sewing the bindings. Patricia Raymond, the Cozy Quilter, accomplished a lot of interesting machine quilting using her long-arm sewing machine, while Katrina Beverage worked her beautiful machine quilting on three of the quilts using her Bernina. Pat Welsh designed and stitched *Wings in Motion* in its entirety.

The book's photography was also a group effort. Sharon Risedorph photographed the flat quilt shots, and Ross Chandler did the portrait photography. Valori Wells, my talented daughter, photographed the quilts on location in Sisters, assisted by stylist Barbara Ferguson. Conklin Guest House, Sisters Antiques, Three Creeks Building, and Richard's Produce graciously allowed us to photograph in their lovely settings, and Dusty Rose contributed a beautiful bouquet of flowers. Diane Pedersen of C&T Publishing took the fabric and close-up shots.

Making the book happen fell to Candie Frankel, my developmental and technical editor, who shared in my vision for its content and lent many ideas, skills, and advice as we developed the manuscript. Christina Jarumay, my design and book director, took the words, photographs, and graphics and once again made them work for my readers in a beautiful way. To both of you, and the editorial and production staff at C&T, my thanks.

Most of all, I am indebted to my husband, John, who always supports me in my endeavors.

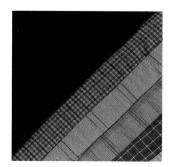

TABLE

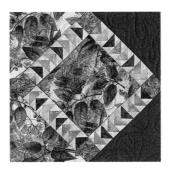

CHAPTER **4** Stars & Points...**85**

CHAPTER **5** Combination Blocks...**103**

OF...

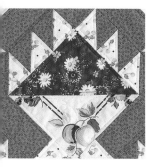

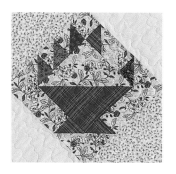

CHAPTER 6 Small Triangles...117

CHAPTER 7 Picture Blocks...133

CHAPTER 8 Free-Form Piecing...151

FOREWORD

This delightful revised edition of *Patchwork Quilts Made Easy* truly does
live up to its title. Jean Wells is known and loved throughout the quilting
world, and she provides a complete and comprehensive approach to today's
quiltmaking experience. Her thirty-plus years of quilting expertise fill every page,
from her discussions about color and fabrics to the many different blocks and quilt
projects she has selected. It is as if Jean is providing private lessons just for you!

Jean has long been interested in both the creative and the practical aspects of
quiltmaking, and how to strike a balance between the two. For the beginner, Jean
gives all the necessary information to get started, such as how to use a rotary cutter, how to sew a perfect one-quarter-inch seam allowance, and how to size half-
and quarter-square triangles. Experienced quilters will find tips and insights that
push their skills and creativity to a new level. True to her own nature, Jean teaches
and expects all of her students to look at the world with open eyes, to be aware of
colors, textures, and designs that turn up in everyday life, and then to experiment
with and translate their discoveries to their quiltmaking.

Jean has taught both myself and thousands of quilters just how much our craft is
to be treasured. Her generous personality and ability
to instruct have formed today's quiltmaker. This
updated volume provides yet more inspiration and
information for us to draw on.

Thank you, Jean, for encouraging and
mentoring my quilting career. Your words
of wisdom and encouragement, I treasure.
It has been an honor to work and play with
you all these years.

Alex Anderson

WELCOME TO SISTERS

In my twenty-seven years as a quiltmaker and owner of The Stitchin' Post, my quilt shop in Sisters, Oregon, I have worked with thousands of students and customers. The never-ending array of projects that I get to see and help move to the final stages of completion is very gratifying.

Living in the small mountain community of Sisters with its snowcapped mountains, tall pine trees, and my casual garden has been a wonderful environment for me to develop my quilting skills, grow my business, and explore color and design.

The second Saturday of July each year, Sisters celebrates quilting with an Outdoor Quilt Show. A thousand quilts hang from porches and buildings and drape over fences in our 1880s-style Western town. Quilting is an integral part of my small community. Thousands of visitors come to the quilt show and The Stitchin' Post every year.

Teaching the sampler quilt class at The Stitchin' Post is one of my very favorite jobs. I look forward to each new group of students eager to partake in the process of making a quilt. I structure the class as a comprehensive experience in techniques, color and design theory, and some history. I want my students to finish the sessions with enough knowledge and experience to have the confidence to tackle most any quilting project. I want them to be successful on their own.

16 PATCHWORK QUILTS MADE EASY

If you can't make it to Oregon, don't despair. *Patchwork Quilts Made Easy* is my way of bringing The Stitchin' Post's sampler class directly to you. Writing books has been a teaching tool for me, and I hope this book will become a learning tool for you—the next best thing to taking a class personally.

We'll start off talking about colors and fabrics and how to choose combinations that work together to make a successful, harmonious palette. If you are new to quilting, you will learn the techniques for cutting and sewing that assure accuracy and a quilt you can be proud of. If you are more experienced, you'll find the book is full of quilt design ideas and inspiration as well as a chance to brush up on technique.

Each project chapter concentrates on a particular aspect of quilting, such as strip piecing or triangles. Illustrated block and quilt instructions make it easy for you to try out these designs. The final chapter features three sampler quilts that use blocks from the entire book. You can start anywhere you like—with a sampler quilt or one of the easier repeat block quilts. There are enough designs here to give you many hours of quilting pleasure. I hope that *Patchwork Quilts Made Easy* will help you develop your own feel for color, pattern, and design in the quilts that you sew. Enjoy!

CHAPTER 1

Quiltmaking Basics

Planning a Quilt

Materials & Equipment

Cutting & Sewing

Planning a Quilt

The first thing most people notice about a quilt is its color. The next time you walk through a quilt show, see if this isn't true for you. Color sets the mood. Bright color combinations grab you and pull you in. Subtle combinations calm you. Rich, earthy combinations are warm and inviting. The right colors can create a sense of time, place, or season. It isn't hard to picture a day at the lake when viewing *Summer Pines* (page 63) with its Log Cabin blocks and pine tree border. Colors have power!

When I was planning this updated edition of *Patchwork Quilts Made Easy*, I envisioned a collection of quilts that would stimulate your creative juices and inspire you in your own search for color palettes. All people have an intuitive color sense, whether they know it or not. Most beginners just lack confidence to try out their ideas. Color speaks directly to us and gets us emotionally involved. Personal experiences that are locked in our memories play a big part in how we react to color. Sometimes we know exactly why we like a particular color, but other times the reason remains a mystery, even to ourselves. Begin with your own responses to color, but be open to expanding your ideas and increasing your sensitivity. Pay attention to the color choices you and others make, and learn as much as you can.

How, exactly, do you go about choosing colors for a quilt? One of the first things I tell my sampler class students is that they need to imagine each potential fabric as "auditioning" for the quilt. How each fabric performs, both on its own and with the other fabrics, will determine whether or not it gets a part. Some fabrics won't be right and will have to wait for the next quilt. When you objectively audition your fabrics, there's less chance of getting so emotionally committed to one fabric that you miss seeing other choices that are better.

Working with color requires close observation. You really have to concentrate and put yourself in the mood of seeking possibilities. Study quilts in books and on display at quilt shops, and learn from other quilter's tastes. Become a student of color. Take note of your surroundings. Look closely at spring flowers or autumn leaves. Take in the winter landscape and memorize the impression it leaves on your mind. Pay attention to the way colors change with the seasons of the year and the time of day.

All color schemes begin somewhere. A Mother's Day card with a beautiful landscape, a snapshot of an early morning sunrise reflecting on the mountains, an advertisement showing a car in the wilderness (minus the car), a painting from your grandson—any of these can become sources of color ideas and combinations that you can use in your quiltmaking.

Toss your favorite pictures and photos in a file box, and glance through them whenever you need inspiration. Remember, color is a way to express your creativity. Color sense is in all of us. It can be brought to life and encouraged to blossom through experience, awareness, and study. When you become a student of color, a whole new world will open up to you.

A photograph of a newly opened poppy inspired this magenta and blue-green fabric palette.

THE PROPORTION RULE

In this exercise, you'll let a colorful bouquet of flowers inspire the palette for a quilt. Here's where you get to play detective. Study your bouquet, and jot down the names of the colors that you see. Use your list to assemble a small group of fabrics. I chose white, purple, a multicolor print, yellow, and green for my palette.

Now go one step further. What percentage of the palette is white? Purple? Yellow? As you study your bouquet closely, you'll find that some colors predominate and others serve more as accents or fillers. Colors that seem the most vivid and prominent may in fact make up a very small percentage of the total palette.

I call this principle the Proportion Rule, and you can apply it to any quilt you are making. In a successful color scheme, one color will dominate. It doesn't matter if the quilt pattern is a Log Cabin, a Sawtooth Star, or some other design. What matters is how much of each color the eye sees. A quilt that is evenly divided, say 50% red and 50% blue, will make you feel unsettled and confused because, subconsciously, you cannot decide whether the quilt is red or blue. Adding a mere one-inch border in one of the colors is enough to tip the color scales and resolve the conflict, making the quilt easier to look at.

Keep the Proportion Rule in mind when you are buying fabric off the bolt. Bolts of fabric look pretty much the same when viewed side by side on a shelf. Sometimes you need to move them around or view a small section of fabric to see the color proportions more clearly. You might be surprised by the results. I used to avoid certain colors because I didn't care for them. The Proportion Rule, along with auditioning, showed me how effective those colors could be in small doses.

The fabric swatches closer to the bouquet represent the overall color palette. The swatches underneath show the same colors in proportion to one another.

PROPERTIES OF COLOR

As quiltmakers, we have a special reason for wanting to understand more about color. A patchwork block is made by sewing different fabric shapes together to create a design. For the design to show up clearly, there has to be **CONTRAST** between the main pattern pieces and the background pieces. Let's look at some basic color properties to better understand what contrast is all about.

First, there is **VALUE**. Value is the lightness or darkness of a color. A color becomes lighter if you add white to it and darker if you add black. The contrast of light, medium, and dark fabrics in a quilt helps define the shapes and keeps the quilt interesting. *Summer Fun* (page 107) is a quilt with high value contrast. See how the light and dark shapes are clear and sharp? For a softer look, compare *Nostalgic Nine-Patch* (page 110). The changes in value are more subtle and the blocks seem to flow together.

If you are uncertain how much—or how little—contrast there is between your fabric choices, cut small swatches and make a photocopy of them. The photocopier reduces fabrics to their black and white values, and you'll know immediately which ones read lighter or darker. Fabric colors that seem different to you, such as red and green, may turn out to be

A green batik and a red batik. The colors are different, but the values are the same.

exactly the same value. In a quilt, this red and green would mix together, and when viewed from a distance, the individual patchwork shapes would be hard to make out.

Here's a value test I do when I'm working at home. I cut a few pieces of each fabric I'm considering and stick them onto a piece of white flannel I have taped to the wall. Then I walk to the other side of the room, turn around, and quickly glance back to see how they strike me. Trust that first impression! If your colors run together and look boring, try another combination. If one fabric sticks out like a sore thumb, change it.

Squinting at the fabrics from across the room or using a reducing glass are two more ways to discern their value. A reducing glass looks like a magnifying glass, but performs exactly the opposite function, letting you see fabrics and quilts as if they were far away. Inexpensive reducing glasses are available at most quilting shops.

Another way to create contrast is with **INTENSITY**. Intensity is the amount of saturation in a color. Think of the vibrancy of true red. Mixing in a small amount of true blue creates brilliant magenta. Really intense colors like these act as bright highlights, especially when they appear among a palette of duller, more subdued colors. Just a small amount is needed to create energizing contrast. On the other hand, you might want to make a quilt like *Harmony* (page 54), which uses lots of intense colors.

Light to dark values of the color purple

Intense colors stand out.

Warm colors

A third way to achieve contrast is by **TEMPERATURE**. Temperature is the quality of the color that affects us emotionally. Any color can be described as warm or cool. Yellows are generally thought of as bright, warm, and intense, yet some yellows are as cool as lemon sherbet. Blue-greens feel warmer than blues containing white or violet. Any color can take on a warm or cool tone depending on what it is mixed with.

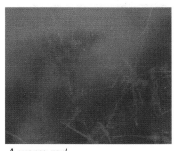

A warm red

A cool red

Cool colors

A warm green

A cool green

In a quilt, warmer colors advance toward you and the spaces they fill appear larger. Cooler colors recede into the background and appear smaller. Each color radiates its own temperature, which in turn affects how the colors around it are perceived.

SELECTING THE FABRIC

When you choose fabrics for a quilt, you're not only dealing with color. You're also considering pattern and style. Fabric can be cute, contemporary, elegant, country, or whimsical in spirit. There are literally thousands of fabrics to choose from, and the mood or style of each fabric you select contributes to the overall design of your quilt. Deciding which fabrics to place side by side in a quilt is part of the auditioning process.

Here are some popular fabric categories:

■ **THEME PRINTS** can take on any character imaginable. Motifs run from juvenile to sophisticated. You can find theme prints depicting animals, plants, holidays, sports, architecture, hobbies, professions, and more.

■ **FLORALS** can come across as delicate and meadowlike, or big and bold. Some look like Impressionist paintings; others suggest Victorian bouquets. Tiny floral calicoes say "traditional."

■ **CHECKS** and **PLAIDS** suggest a casual country look. They can be woven or printed. Printed checks are especially whimsical.

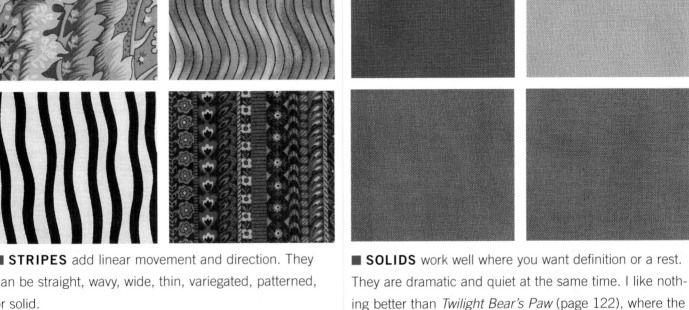

■ **STRIPES** add linear movement and direction. They can be straight, wavy, wide, thin, variegated, patterned, or solid.

■ **SOLIDS** work well where you want definition or a rest. They are dramatic and quiet at the same time. I like nothing better than *Twilight Bear's Paw* (page 122), where the all-solid palette creates sharp, clear lines.

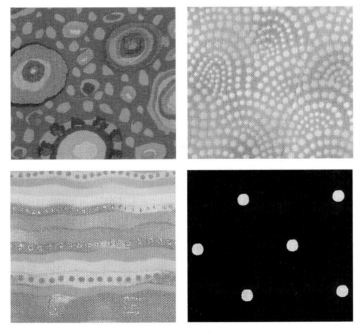

■ **GEOMETRICS** bring swirling movement or architectural precision to the quilt. Circles, dots, triangles, zigzags, radiating designs, and other abstract shapes fall into this category.

■ **TEXTURED SOLIDS**, or **BLENDERS**, are low-contrast two-color prints or monochromatic prints. When viewed from a distance, blenders come across as areas of subtle texture. In many quilts, they add more interest than a true solid would.

When you audition fabrics, you may find that the colors are working but something else seems off. The problem may be one of **SCALE**. For good visual texture, or contrast, the sizes of the designs printed on the fabrics should vary. Let's say you started with a theme fabric that

Large-scale prints

■ **BATIKS** have a sharp, bright, contemporary feel. This is because the dyeing is done over a tightly woven base cloth, with more threads to the inch than is typical for quilting cottons.

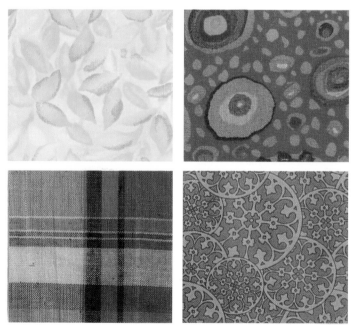

Medium-scale prints and plaid

■ **FLANNELS** have a fuzzy, soft surface that is perfect for baby quilts. Plaids and outdoorsy theme prints lend themselves to men's projects.

has a large print. To vary the scale, you might add one or two small prints that read as overall texture from a distance, with a medium-scale print and maybe a plaid to draw them together.

Small-scale prints

Another factor to consider is the **SPACING BETWEEN MOTIFS**. Florals can have a packed-together tight look, they can be open and airy, or they can appear in clusters. If you are using several florals, a combination of "tight" and "loose" can help create contrast. Florals can be tricky to use. Always view a floral print from a distance to make sure you like the effect. You may find that some flowers lose their detail and appear like splotches of color—the exact opposite of the look you're trying to create.

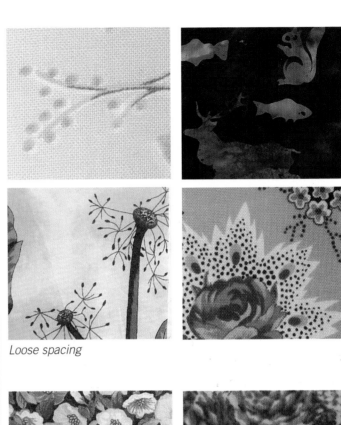

Loose spacing

Tight spacing

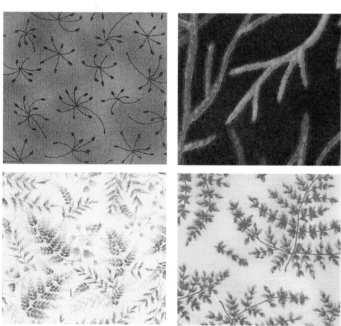

Clustered prints

Not too tight or too loose

Also look at **MOVEMENT**, or the way a printed fabric draws the eye around. There might be a lot of movement, or very little. Study the print. Is it a textured solid that will read almost as a solid from a distance? Or does it have bold contrast? Swirling or circular patterns will carry the eye along with them. If a print is large, and you need to use just a part of it, cut a window the same size as the template from a piece of paper. Then move the paper window frame over the print so that you can see the different cutting options.

Using a window template

PUTTING IT ALL TOGETHER

I like the journey aspect of the quilting process—picking my fabrics, planning the design, and then making it all come together. Sometimes I think about a quilt and collect fabric for it over a long period of time. It is fun and satisfying to pick up little pieces here and there. The collecting becomes part of the story that the quilt has to tell.

Once you've made some basic decisions about your quilt design, don't rush out to go fabric shopping. Instead, pull fabrics from your stash at home. You never know what you might come across that could make your quilt better. Work within your idea but stay flexible. Take your time shopping for and assembling your fabric palette.

Using a Theme Fabric

Many fabric companies design groups of fabrics that coordinate with each other. Usually, a collection features a single theme fabric along with coordinates or extractions. An extraction is a smaller print based on one or more of the theme motifs. Your job is made easier if you pick the whole group, but sometimes the look is just too predictable. Your quilt will be more interesting and personal if you toss in fabrics from other manufacturers.

To choose your own palette at the fabric store, I suggest holding the bolt of theme fabric horizontally and walking alongside the shelves of fabric, pulling any that seem to work with the theme. Once you have a group of fabrics assembled, begin a process of elimination. This method of auditioning forces you to view more fabrics than you will need. You'll stay open to new possibilities and also remain more objective. Besides, it's easier to eliminate fabrics than it is to come up with one more fabric to fill a gap.

Don't be overly fussy when you are picking fabrics to audition. When I first opened The Stitchin' Post, people would come in with a piece of fabric and try to match a color that was as small as a $1/8$" dot. They did not realize that such a tiny dot, viewed from a distance, would mix with the color next to it and create a third color. It's better to trust your instincts and evaluate fabric groupings as a whole.

Picking fabrics to audition

More than two dozen fabrics coordinate with this leafy theme print.

How a Palette Develops

When I teach my sampler quilt class, we spend a lot of time talking about fabric. Fabrics need to be "friends." You want the fabrics in your quilt to have something in common. But in any group of friends, isn't there one person who is a little livelier or crazier than the rest? You need this wacky fabric friend to add sparkle to the quilt.

In class, fabrics are introduced to the blocks like characters in a novel. First, you make one-third of your blocks, creating as many different combinations as you want, just like an author invents new characters. At this stage, you may not know who the main character is. Your blocks will not look like they go together because there are no repeated combinations.

When you make a sampler quilt, the color proportions take time to emerge.

To make the next third of your blocks, refer to the first group and find fabrics and combinations to repeat. Introduce subtle fabric changes so that no two blocks are exactly the same.

When two-thirds of the blocks are finished, it's evaluation time. Here's when you take a serious look at the blocks and ask what direction you want the quilt to take. For example, if the blocks are pink, green, and yellow, you might say, "I want the quilt to be more green than pink and to have yellow accents." At this stage, the quilt-in-progress is helping you make decisions about what fabrics to use in the last third of the blocks. When you learn to "please the quilt" in this way, you will have arrived as a quilter. This includes being able to let go of your very favorite fabric when it doesn't work in the group, or perhaps finding new fabric friends that will allow it to stay. In either case, the key is to be objective in your choices.

■ THE ART OF REPETITION

Most quilts use repetitive elements to unify the design. Even subtle repetitions of a fabric, value, or shape serve this function. Here are some ideas to try:
• In a sampler quilt, keep the background color consistent in all the blocks.
• In a set of Log Cabin blocks, use the same red fabric for all the center patches.
• In a set of star blocks, use the same value for all the star points.
• Choose a border fabric that repeats or echoes a color used elsewhere in the quilt.
• Repeat a patchwork or appliqué design in the quilting stitching.

Planning Borders

A border acts like a picture frame. It surrounds the quilt top, unifying and finishing it. The border can be a narrow, one-color strip, or it can be an elaborate, multiple-width addition in different fabrics.

When I am designing a quilt, I find it difficult to determine the border until I am finished piecing. I like to look at the pieced top and ask myself, "What does the quilt need? Does it need a border?" Sometimes the answer is no. *Favorite Quilt* (page 113 and close-up, below) had so much pattern and movement, the design contained itself and kept the eye focused. A black print binding is all the framing that was needed. If the answer is yes, however, my next thoughts are, "What width will complement the design?" and "What color should the border be?" Rather than guess at the answers, I go back into auditioning mode.

When you reach this stage, place the quilt top on a design wall or a table. Open up the fabric you think might work as a border and slip it under one of the corners to get a visual picture of how the quilt will look. Maneuver the border fabric wider or narrower until you find the width that's right. Sometimes, the border I have been visualizing from the beginning just doesn't work, and I end up choosing a different fabric altogether. I never mind going back to the drawing table, because I want the quilt to be the best it can be.

A wide outer border restrains a narrow, bright inner border.

Finding Your Style

As you leaf through the pages in this book, you'll find a wealth of ideas for block and quilt designs, fabric choices, and colors. Use the book for inspiration. If you like a particular design but not the palette, determine where the lights, mediums, and darks fall and substitute your own hues. Somewhere along the way, you will start saying to yourself, "I would have done this," or "I would have changed that." Congratulations! You are starting to develop your own color and design sense. This is what quilting is all about.

A borderless quilt

✦ HOW TO CHANGE THE PALETTE

Changing the palette of a project quilt is easy. First, audition your fabrics to find a combination that you like. Use the Proportion Rule to determine each color's prominence in the quilt, starting with the most prominent. Now look at the materials list for the project quilt. You will see that the fabrics are arranged the same way, from the most prominent down to the least prominent. Simply compare your list to the existing materials list to make the substitutions. For scrappy quilts, think in terms of color families, rather than the exact order of the list. Make a sample block to see if you like the result.

Materials & Equipment

In the previous section, we talked about the creative side of quiltmaking. Now let's switch gears and take a look at the nuts and bolts.

A quilt contains three layers. The top layer can be patchwork, appliqué, or a combination of both. The middle layer is batting—a nonwoven filler material that is usually made of polyester, cotton, or a blend of the two. The backing is a layer of fabric placed under the batting. You might visualize a quilt as a sandwich with a fancy top. Quilting is the process of stitching the three layers together so that the batting doesn't move around and the entire sandwich is stabilized. Quilting may be done by hand or by sewing machine.

To make a quilt, you will need the materials that actually go into the quilt, such as fabric, thread, and batting. The fabric and batting requirements for each quilt project in this book can be found under "Materials" in the quilt instructions. You will also need a sewing machine, an iron, and various sewing tools, some of which are specialized to quiltmaking.

FABRIC

For easier piecing and quilting, use 100% cotton fabrics in a medium broadcloth weight. Cotton fabric is flexible yet takes a press well, and you'll find it has a soft, comfortable hand, or feel, to it. Most fabrics are manufactured with some kind of finish to reduce wrinkling. These finishes generally don't wash out completely, and fabrics that are really stiff probably will not soften up when washed.

Cotton quilting fabric is typically 44" wide, including the selvages, but some fabrics may be slightly narrower. The selvages should never be included in your quilt, since they can pucker and distort the seams. If the selvages look especially troublesome, trim them off at the start to avoid distortion; otherwise, just trim them off as you are cutting the pieces. With the selvages removed, the fabric will measure between $42^1/_2$" and $43^1/_2$" wide. Each quilt project in this book lists the fabric yardage requirements. The listed amounts allow for selvage removal, some shrinkage, and small variations in fabric width, but not a whole lot extra, so plan accordingly.

Before I purchase a fabric, I rub it between my fingers. If the dye comes off, I know it will bleed. Darker fabrics like purples, deep blues, and reds are the most prone to lose dye and bleed. If you are unsure whether a fabric will change size or lose color, wash and dry it ahead of time as you would the finished project. Warm water and detergent are recommended. For flannels, use a cool-water wash, machine-dry on a warm (not hot) setting, and press before using. I like to prewash batiks, Bali prints, and other hand-dyed fabrics with Synthrapol, a liquid wetting agent, to set the colors. If fabrics you have prewashed continue to bleed, don't use them in a quilt.

▒ QUILTER'S TIP

One of my sampler class students came up with this idea: Stitch two 1" x 2" strips of fabric together, one white and one a deep color. Put the piece in water. You will soon see if the darker fabric bleeds.

Make note of the fabric grain, especially if you pretrim the selvages. The lengthwise threads, or straight of grain, run parallel to the selvages. They are strong and have very little give. The crosswise threads run perpendicular to the lengthwise threads and have a bit of stretch when pulled. The bias runs at a 45° angle to the crosswise and lengthwise grains and has the most give. Binding that needs to wrap around curved edges is cut on the bias. Plaids cut on the bias take on a whole new look.

❖ BUILDING A FABRIC STASH

If you enjoy quilting, you will soon be collecting fabrics for future quilts. Planning new palettes is part of the quilting process. If I absolutely love a fabric and think I might want it for a border, I buy 3 yards. When I am unsure how I will use a fabric, I buy a smaller amount, usually ³/₄ yard.

Buying "fat quarters" is a perfect way to build a fabric stash. A fat quarter is ¹/₄ yard of fabric, but it measures 18" x 22" instead of 9" x 44". Fat quarters give you more cutting options for scrap quilts and smaller projects. Instead of a long, narrow rectangle, you're working with a shape that's almost square.

A basket of fat quarters. This warm, summery palette was used to make Fresh Produce *(page 199).*

THREAD

Use **cotton sewing thread** for piecing cotton fabrics. Match the thread to the basic mood of the quilt. For most quilts, I use a dull tan thread. If the quilt is very dark or very light, I change the thread color to match. For appliqué, match the thread color to the appliqué fabric.

For machine quilting, you can use clear **monofilament thread**, also known as invisible thread, or one of the many **colored cotton threads** available for this purpose. Use either of these threads in the top of the machine and a cotton thread that matches the back of the quilt in the bobbin.

For hand quilting, use **quilting thread**, which is stronger than ordinary sewing thread. Quilting thread is traditionally white or cream, but today it is also available in colors, which can add more contrast and interest to your project.

BATTING

Batting choices are practically endless. I try to match the batting to my quilt. Of course, I want cotton or a cotton blend whenever possible because I'm using cotton fabric and thread.

For wall quilts, I prefer thin, flat batting so that the quilt lies flat against the wall. You will be amazed at how clearly the quilting stitches show on even a thin batt.

For bed quilts, I prefer a slightly thicker batting. Polyester loft-type batting will appear puffy at first but will flatten as the quilt is used. Some people like it for children's projects.

TOOLS AND SUPPLIES

Quality tools make a difference.

There are lots of tools and gadgets designed especially for quilters, and you are sure to have your favorites. Always purchase the best equipment you can afford, from your rotary cutter to your marking pencils. Quality equipment will last longer and help you achieve greater accuracy in your work. Here's a list of the essentials.

For Cutting

■ **ROTARY CUTTER.** A rotary cutter has a very sharp round blade mounted on a plastic handle, similar to a pizza cutter. It comes in several sizes. I find larger cutters easier to handle.

■ **CUTTING MAT.** Use a plastic self-healing cutting mat to protect the tabletop during rotary cutting. An 18" x 24" mat is ample.

■ **ROTARY CUTTING RULERS.** Specially designed for quilters, these $1/8$"-thick acrylic see-through grid rulers are marked in 1", $1/2$", $1/4$", and $1/8$" increments. Rotary cutting rulers come in many different sizes. My favorites are 6" x 12", $6^1/2$" x $24^1/2$", and 15" x 15" (for squaring up blocks).

■ **FABRIC SHEARS.** Use these sharp shears for cutting fabric only.

■ **PAPER-CUTTING SCISSORS.** Use these scissors for cutting paper and template plastic.

For Sewing

■ **SEWING MACHINE.** Be sure yours is in good working order.

■ **IRON AND IRONING BOARD.**

■ **MACHINE NEEDLES.** Machine needles for piecing quilts are sized 10/70 to 14/90. The higher the number, the larger the needle. For cotton fabrics, an average-size needle is recommended. Change the needle with every major project since they do get burrs on the side.

■ **HAND NEEDLES.** A #11 sharp needle works well for sewing and appliqué. Milliner's needles are another choice for appliqué. Betweens in size 8, 9, or 10 are used for hand quilting. The higher the number, the smaller the needle.

■ **STRAIGHT PINS.** Flat-head and glass-head pins are easier to see and manipulate than long, thick-shank pins. Flat-head pins let you rest a rotary cutting ruler on top of your pinned fabric. Glass-head pins won't melt under the heat of an iron.

■ **SEAM RIPPER.**

■ **NEEDLE THREADER.** Purchase a threader with a different size wire on each end. Use the finer end to thread tiny quilting or appliqué needles.

■ **BEESWAX.** Run hand quilting thread along a cake of beeswax just before you sew. The light wax coating makes the thread stronger and reduces tangling.

■ **THIMBLE.** Choose a size that fits comfortably on the second finger of your stitching hand.

Miscellaneous

■ **PLASTIC-COATED FREEZER PAPER.** Use plastic-coated freezer paper, available at supermarkets, to make templates for hand appliqué. The shiny side can be ironed directly to the fabric for a firm, temporary hold.

■ **FABRIC STABILIZER.** Use fabric stabilizer whenever you machine-appliqué.

■ **PAPER-BACKED FUSIBLE WEB.** Use fusible web to make no-sew fusible appliqués and buttonhole stitch appliqués.

■ **PENCILS.** Use a hard lead pencil (0.5), silver pencil, or charcoal pencil to mark fabric. Pencil markings normally wash out, but always do a test on your fabric before you begin. You'll also need a pencil sharpener.

■ **⅝"-WIDE MASKING TAPE.** Use this wide tape for quilt basting.

■ **¼"-WIDE MASKING TAPE.** Use this narrow tape to mark quilting lines for hand quilting.

■ **TAPE MEASURE.**

■ **MEDIUM-SIZE SAFETY PINS.** Use safety pins to baste the quilt layers together.

■ **QUILTING HOOP.** Use a 14" to 18" hoop for hand quilting.

Cutting & Sewing

The techniques involved in making a quilt are not difficult, but it is important to learn how to do them properly and accurately from the beginning. This section provides an overview of the quiltmaking process, from cutting the first patch to sewing on the binding. You'll also find basic techniques for appliqué. If you are a beginning quilter, start by reading this chapter and practicing some of the techniques. When you're ready to make a quilt, follow the project instructions in the chapters that follow and refer back to this chapter whenever you are unsure how to do something.

Always rotary-cut from a standing position.

ROTARY CUTTING

The rotary cutter is such a fast, efficient way to cut fabric, most quilt instructions written today assume you will be using one. In rotary cutting, the fabric is cut across the grain, from selvage to selvage, to make strips. Then the strips are cut into squares, rectangles, or triangles. The individual quilt instructions will tell you how wide to cut the strips, how many strips to cut, and what smaller shapes to cut.

Begin by placing your cutting mat on a table so that you can stand over it while you cut. A standing position will be more comfortable and allow you to exert firm, consistent pressure on the rotary cutter. The instructions that follow are for right-handed cutting. If you are left-handed, reverse the orientation.

Cutting a Straight Edge

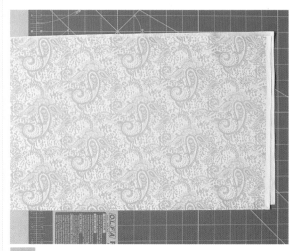

1 Fold the fabric in half, right side out. Match the selvages as closely as possible.

2 Bring the folded edge almost to the selvages and fold again, so that the entire piece is resting on the cutting mat and the selvages are in a double layer on the far right.

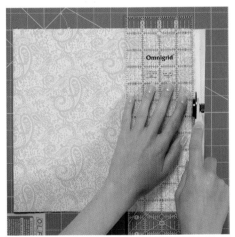

3 Place a long cutting ruler on the fabric to the left of the selvages, aligning it as best you can. Make sure that the first fold is under the ruler and that only two layers of fabric lie to the right of the ruler. Adjust as necessary. Place the fingers of your left hand on the ruler, safely clear of the right edge of the ruler, and hold down firmly. Depress the safety latch on the rotary cutter. Place the rotary

blade on the fabric at the lower right corner of the ruler. Roll the cutter along the right edge of the ruler, away from yourself and toward and slightly past the top edge of the fabric. Press firmly but not too heavily. When the cut is complete, put the safety latch back on the blade. (Get in the habit of doing this after every cut.)

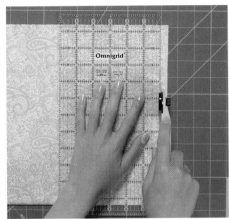

4 Rotate the cutting mat one quarter turn to the left, or in a counterclockwise direction. Place a 6" x 12" ruler on the fabric, aligning the 6" edge parallel to the trimmed selvage edge. Move the ruler as far as you can to the right and still have four layers of fabric under it. Hold down the ruler with your left hand, depress the safety latch on the rotary cutter, and glide the cutter along the ruler edge from bottom to top, or away from yourself. You now have a straight edge to begin your strip cutting. Repeat steps 1–4 for each new piece of fabric that you cut.

Strips

1 Cut a straight edge as described. Rotate the cutting mat 180° (or walk around the table) so that the straight-cut edge is now at the left side of the fabric. You will be measuring and cutting strips from the left edge of the fabric.

2 To make a 4$\frac{1}{2}$" x 42" strip, align the 4$\frac{1}{2}$" mark of the ruler on the left edge of the fabric. Make sure the 6" edges of the ruler are parallel to the folded edge and the pretrimmed selvages. Double-check that the fabric that appears under the ruler matches the required strip width.

3 To make the cut, press the ruler firmly against the fabric with your entire left hand, release the safety latch with your right hand, and glide the cutter against the right edge of the ruler. Always start the cut at the bottom and roll away from yourself.

Squares

A strip is easily cut into squares. For a $4^1/2$" square, start with a $4^1/2$"-wide strip. Open up the strip of fabric. Align the $4^1/2$" mark of the ruler on the $4^1/2$" cut edge. Make sure the 6" edges of the ruler run parallel to the long edges of the strip. Double-check that the fabric that appears under the ruler is the required size and shape and then make the cut. If your project requires multiple squares, you may stack up to four strips for cutting.

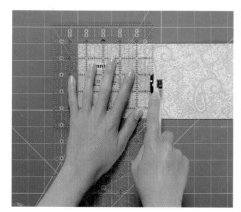

Cutting a $4^1/2$" square

⊠ QUILTER'S TIP

To stay organized, stack your cut fabric pieces and label them with sticky notes. Arrange the pieces in the order they will be stitched.

Half-Square Triangles

To make half-square triangles, start with a square. Lay the ruler diagonally across the block, from corner to corner, and make a cut. You can stack up to four squares to make multiples. (For larger amounts, try the paper method described on page 77).

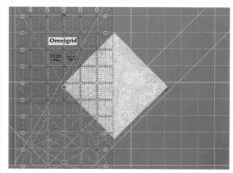

Align the ruler

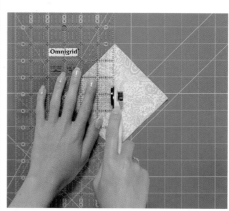

Cut from corner to corner

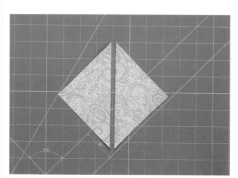

Two half-square triangles

Quarter-Square Triangles

To make quarter-square triangles, cut a square diagonally in both directions. Each square makes four triangles.

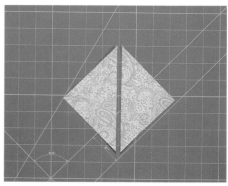

Cut in half

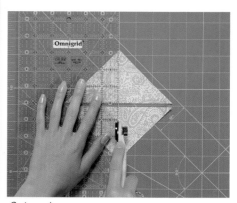

Cut again

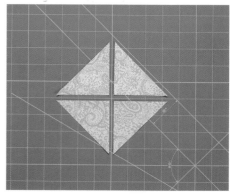

Four quarter-square triangles

MAKING AND USING TEMPLATES

Some quilt blocks use shapes that are cut with templates. These include geometric shapes, such as the roof and sky pieces in *Pinebrook* (page 140), and appliqués, such as the bunnies in *Rabbit Patch* (page 180).

Reusable templates can be made of template plastic, available in quilt shops. This thin plastic sheet looks milky but still allows see-through. Lay the plastic over the pattern printed in the book and trace all the marked lines with a pencil or a fine-point marking pen. Use a ruler to draft straight lines accurately. Cut out the template with scissors.

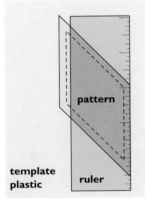

Making a Plastic Template

To use a plastic template, place it on the fabric and trace around it with a sharp pencil. Cut out the fabric shape, using a rotary cutter and ruler to cut straight edges and fabric shears to cut curved edges. In this book, the patchwork template patterns include a $^1/_4$" seam allowance, but the appliqué template patterns do not, so be sure to follow the individual quilt instructions for cutting.

Sometimes you will use a template to cut two or more shapes, half of them in mirror image. Fold the fabric right side in, mark the template outline, and then cut through both layers for two mirror image pieces. Another method is to layer up to four fabrics right side up, cut the required pieces, and then flip the template over to cut the reverse shapes.

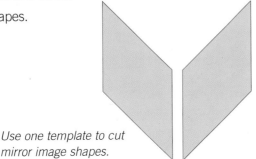

Use one template to cut mirror image shapes.

SEWING AND PIECING

"Piecing" means sewing various patchwork shapes together to make a quilt block and then joining the blocks into a quilt top. Because a quilt contains so many seams, accuracy is critical. If you stitch a seam even a couple of threads off, the problems add up and the block will be too large or too small. Fortunately, accuracy and efficiency go hand in hand when it comes to quilting.

The $^1/_4$" Seam Allowance

In quiltmaking all seams are sewn with a $^1/_4$" seam allowance. The block size refers to the finished dimensions, without the seam allowance factored in. Keep this in mind as you work. If you are making a 12" block, it should actually measure $12^1/_2$" x $12^1/_2$", or 12" x 12" plus a $^1/_4$" seam allowance all around.

To sew an accurate $^1/_4$" seam, the sewing machine needle must enter the fabric exactly $^1/_4$" from the fabric edge. On some machines, the right edge of the presser foot is exactly $^1/_4$" from the needle. You simply line up the cut edge of the fabric with the edge of the foot to sew an accurate $^1/_4$" seam. Another option is to use a marking on the machine's throat plate as a guide. To determine which is accurate for your machine, draw a line on a piece of paper $^1/_4$" from the cut edge (or use $^1/_4$" graph paper). Place the paper on the machine's throat plate, cut edge to the right, and lower the needle so that it passes through the marked line. Then lower the presser foot. The right edge of the paper indicates the $^1/_4$" mark. If it does not align with the foot, apply a piece of masking tape to the throat plate even with the paper edge. For a slightly raised marker, substitute a thin piece of Moleskin foot and shoe padding for the tape.

Measure for the seam allowance with ¼" graph paper.

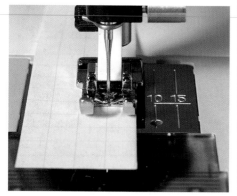

Using a ¼" presser foot as a guide

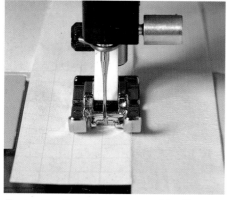

Taping the throat plate as a guide. Be careful not to tape over the feed dogs.

Chaining

If you are making multiple quilt blocks, the work will go faster if you stitch all of the smaller units together at one time. This technique is called chaining.

1 Set the machine stitch length at 14 to 16 stitches to the inch.

2 Feed the first pair of layered pieces through the machine, stitching them together.

3 As you near the end of the stitching line, pick up the next pair to be joined. Without lifting the presser foot, feed this pair through the machine. Repeat until all of the pieces are stitched.

4 Remove the chain from the machine. Use scissors to clip the threads between the pairs.

Chaining Triangles

⊞ NO MORE BUNCHING

Here's a tip to get your chain off to a good start. Fold a 1" x 2" scrap of fabric in half. Lower the presser foot and take a few stitches through the scrap fabric before feeding through the other pieces. The scrap fabric will give you a handle at the rear and prevent the threads from bunching up. Use another scrap at the end of the chain to keep your last few stitches from wandering off course.

PRESSING

Pressing is very important in any sewing project. In patchwork, there are several rules to remember:

■ Use a dry iron.

■ Press as you go.

■ Press both seam allowances toward the darker fabric.

■ If two seams will meet, press them in opposite directions. This way, the seams will nest together during stitching and the points will match. Do this even if it means breaking the "darker fabric" rule.

■ Press up and down the seam, not from side to side, to avoid stretching and distorting the fabric pieces.

■ After a block is completed, apply spray fabric finish to the surface and press again. This finish (not the same as spray starch) is available at supermarkets and hardware stores. It helps the fabric hold a press better.

APPLIQUÉ

Appliquéd quilt blocks are made by applying cutout shapes to a background fabric. If you've never appliquéd before, I suggest starting with a heart shape (use the pattern on page 80). Appliqué can be done by machine, by hand, or by fusing.

Machine Appliqué

For machine appliqué, use cotton thread or machine embroidery thread, both of which fill in better than polyester thread. A stabilizer underneath the background fabric will prevent puckering and hold everything in place as you sew. A stabilizer looks like nonwoven interfacing. After you sew through it, just tear it away and discard it. I used typing paper before this product was developed but find that stabilizer works much better.

1 Cut the appliqué the same size as the printed pattern. Position the appliqué on the background fabric, right sides up. Cut a piece of stabilizer the same size as the background fabric and place it underneath the background. Cut a few pieces of scrap fabric and stabilizer for test purposes.

2 Set the zigzag stitch to almost its full $1/16$" width. Set the stitch length to fine, so the threads will fall close together and form a satiny look. You will need to position the work on the machine so that the needle hits just outside the appliqué shape. Test the stitch on the scrap pieces and make any needed adjustments. Refer to your sewing machine manual for further instructions.

3 Begin stitching on a straight edge of the appliqué. As you reach a curve or rounded area, don't force the fabric to turn. It will turn gently on its own with a little guidance from you. Learning to feed the fabric and letting it flow gently are the keys to smooth stitching.

4 At an inside point, stitch into the notch for one stitch width and stop with the needle in the down position. Lift the presser foot and turn the fabric; then lower the foot and continue.

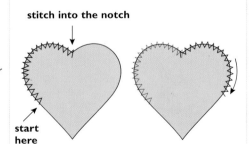

stitch into the notch

start here

5 After a shape is appliquéd, you may wish to topstitch details shown on the pattern. When all the stitching is complete, tear off the excess stabilizer.

Hand Appliqué

There are several ways to hand-appliqué. In the needleturn method that I teach beginners, the freezer paper template goes on top of the appliqué and serves as a guide for folding in the edge. You'll use your needle to turn under the edge as you go.

1 Lay a piece of freezer paper, shiny side down, on the appliqué pattern. Trace the pattern outline, and cut out the shape. Make one freezer paper cutout for each appliqué.

2 Lay the appliqué fabric right side up. Place the freezer paper cutout, shiny side down, on top. Press with a warm dry iron until the cutout adheres.

3 Cut the fabric $3/16$" beyond the cutout shape all around. Clip any inside points as needed.

clip into the notch

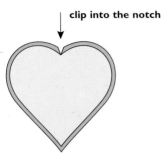

4 Lay the background fabric right side up. Position the appliqué, paper side up, on top. Pin from the wrong side. (This way, you won't catch the appliqué thread on the pins.)

5 Cut an 18" length of thread in a color that matches the appliqué. Thread one end into an appliqué or milliner's needle and knot the other end. Start on a straight edge of the appliqué. Turn under the seam allowance for about 1" with your fingertips.

turn under
raw edge

6 To begin stitching, bring the needle up from the underside, catching the folded edge of the appliqué. Draw the thread through to the right side. Insert the needle into the same spot through the background fabric only. Come out about $1/8$" away, once again catching the folded edge of the appliqué, and draw the thread through. This method of sewing is

called blindstitching. The stitches should be barely visible.

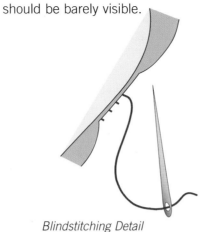

Blindstitching Detail

7 Continue sewing, using your needle to turn under the edge just ahead of your stitching. Along a curve, run your needle underneath the entire stretch to distribute the seam allowance evenly. Keep the threads on the back of the fabric no more than $1/8$" apart. At an inside point, run the needle along the fabric edge to pull the threads underneath. Tack at the very center. As you come to an outside point, fold in the tip first, and then fold in the sides.

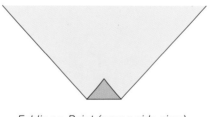

Folding a Point (wrong side view)

8 When the appliquéing is complete, carefully peel off the freezer paper.

Fusible Appliqué

Appliqués can also be attached by fusing. You will need an iron and paper-backed fusible web. Hand or machine stitching can be added around the edges. If you plan to add a decorative edging, be sure to choose a sewable web for easy needling.

1 Lay the fusible web, paper side up, on the appliqué pattern. Trace the pattern outline.

Trace

2 Cut out the shape about ¹/₄"
beyond the marked line. The cutting
does not have to be precise.

Rough-cut

3 Lay the appliqué fabric facedown.
Place the cutout, web side down, on
the fabric. Fuse in place, following
the manufacturer's instructions.

Fuse

4 Cut out the appliqué on the
marked line.

Cut out

5 Peel off the paper backing. Lay
the background fabric right side up.
Position the appliqué right side up on
top, and fuse in place. Thread two or
three strands of floss in an embroidery
needle, and work a hand buttonhole
stitch around the edges. The edges
can also be stitched by machine,
using either hemstitch or a narrow
zigzag stitch. For machine stitching,
use monofilament thread or cotton
thread that matches the appliqué in
the top of the machine and cotton
thread in the bobbin.

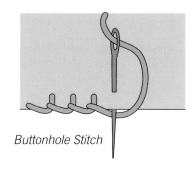

Buttonhole Stitch

ASSEMBLING THE QUILT TOP

Each quilt in this book includes a
diagram that shows how to arrange
the blocks, borders, and other pieces
that make up the quilt top. Follow the
individual project instructions to cut
the required pieces. To make long
sashing or border strips, stitch shorter
strips together on the diagonal until
you have the required length.

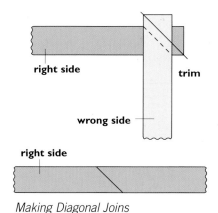

Making Diagonal Joins

Straight Set

In a straight set, the blocks are
arranged in horizontal rows and/or
vertical columns. Sometimes pieced
or appliquéd blocks alternate with
plain blocks. In addition to the
blocks, the set may include sashing
strips and squares. The *Scrap Basket*
quilt diagram (page 80) is an example
of a straight set. The *Oregon Trail*
quilt diagram (page 121) shows a
straight set with sashing.

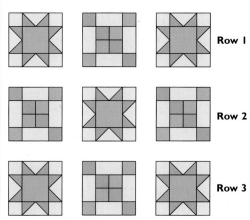

Straight Set

Follow the quilt instructions to stitch the blocks and any other pieces together, using a $1/4$" seam allowance for all seams. Press the seam allowances in one direction on odd-numbered rows and in the opposite direction on even-numbered rows. Then join row 2 to row 1, row 3 to row 2, and so on. When you join the rows, the seam allowances that you pressed in opposite directions will automatically nest together.

Diagonal Set

In a diagonal set, square blocks are set on point and the rows run across the quilt at a 45° angle. Setting triangles fill in around the edges and at the corners. The blocks may be joined directly to one another or they may be separated by sashing strips and squares. The *Springtime Meadow* quilt diagram (page 59) is an example of a diagonal set. The *Primarily Stars* quilt diagram (page 98) shows a diagonal set with sashing.

To complete a diagonal set quilt top, stitch the blocks, sashing (if any), and setting triangles together in diagonal rows. Press the seam allowances in one direction on the odd-numbered rows and in the other direction on even-numbered rows. Join the rows together, nesting the seams. Add the corner triangles last.

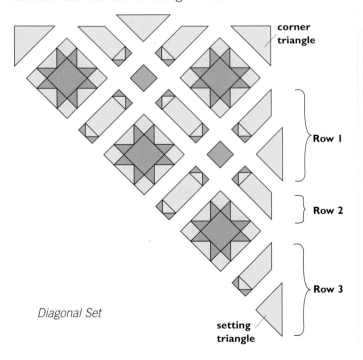

corner triangle

Row 1

Row 2

Row 3

Diagonal Set

setting triangle

CHANGING THE SIZE OF A QUILT

Any quilt in this book can easily be made larger or smaller by adding or subtracting blocks. Measure your bed and decide on the drop, or how far you want the quilt to hang down on the sides. Then add or subtract blocks accordingly to reach the desired dimensions.

Let's say you'd like to enlarge *Favorite Quilt* (page 113) to fit a 60" x 80" queen-sized bed. The original quilt is $60^1/2$" x $72^1/2$", the blocks are 12" square, and the set is 5 blocks wide x 6 blocks long, or 30 blocks total. If the set were enlarged to 8 blocks x 8 blocks, or 64 blocks total, the new dimensions would be $96^1/2$" x $96^1/2$", or enough for an 18" drop around three sides of the bed. The difference between the block totals—34 blocks in this example—is the number of additional blocks needed. If a quilt has sashing or borders, factor them into your calculations.

COMMON MATTRESS SIZES

Crib	27" x 52"
Twin	39" x 75"
Full	54" x 75"
Queen	60" x 80"
King	76" x 80"

QUILTER'S TIP

Keep your finished quilt blocks flat and clean by storing them in an unused pizza box. Purchase an empty box from your local pizza parlor. Label the box with a heavy black felt-tip pen so your family doesn't accidentally throw the box away.

Straight Borders

Cut the border strips for your quilt to the exact measurements given in the cutting instructions. Lay a side border strip on the quilt top, right sides together, and pin. Make sure any seam allowances along the quilt edge stay in the direction you originally pressed them. With the back of the quilt top facing up, stitch $1/4$" from the pinned edges. Press the seam allowance toward the border. Join the opposite side border strip and press. Add the top and bottom border strips in the same way. Press these seam allowances toward the border too. If the quilt has several borders, follow the same procedure for each one.

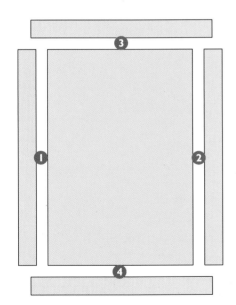

Straight Border Assembly

Add the borders in the order shown

Mitered Corner Borders

Mitered border strips are cut larger than needed, and the excess is trimmed off during the mitering process. To determine the cut length, measure the edge of the quilt top and add two border widths plus 5". For example, if you are sewing a 4"-wide border to 48" edge, the cut length of the strip would be 48" + 4" + 4" + 5", or 61". Once the four strips are cut, here's how to proceed:

1 Use pins to mark the midpoint of one edge of the quilt top and the corresponding border strip. Place the strip on the quilt top, right sides together and matching the pins. Pin from the center out to each edge, letting the excess strip extend evenly at each end. Machine-stitch with a $1/4$" seam allowance, backstitching $1/4$" from the edge of the quilt top at each end. Press the seam allowance toward the border strip.

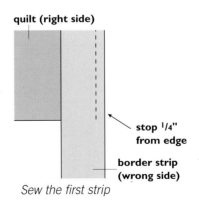

quilt (right side)

stop $1/4$" from edge

border strip (wrong side)

Sew the first strip

2 Repeat step 1 on the adjacent edge of the quilt top. This time, end the backstitching at the seam line. Press the seam allowance toward the border.

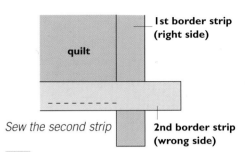

quilt

1st border strip (right side)

Sew the second strip

2nd border strip (wrong side)

3 Lay the quilt top right side up., so that the border strips overlap at a right angle. Fold the top border strip under itself, even with the strip underneath, to form a 45° angle.

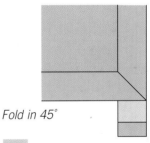

Fold in 45°

4 Use a right-angle triangle or grid ruler to check the angle and confirm that the corner is square. Adjust as needed. Press to set the crease.

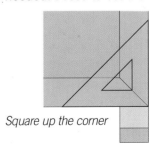

Square up the corner

❖ QUILTER'S TIP

On large quilts, use a pin to mark the midpoint of each border strip and each quilt edge. Match up the pins so that the fabric is distributed evenly along the length of the strip. If any easing is necessary, it will be evenly divided along the border's edge.

5 Fold the entire quilt top diagonally, right side in, bringing the long edges of the border strips together. Pin the border strips together along the pressed-in crease. Stitch along the crease line from the inside corner to the outside corner, backstitching at each end. Be careful not to stretch the fabric. Trim off the excess border strip ¼" beyond the stitching. Press the seam open.

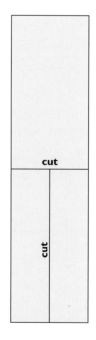

Stitch on the crease

6 Repeat steps 2–5 until all four corners are mitered.

FINISHING A QUILT

Marking the Quilting Design

There are a number of ways to mark a quilting design, should you wish to go that route. Pencil lines, drawn lightly, work fine, but do test your pencil marks on a scrap of fabric first to make sure they will wash out. Pencil marks are more likely to remain in fabrics that have not been prewashed. Heat will set most pencil marks, so avoid pressing the quilt top until the marks are removed. If marks prove stubborn, try a fabric eraser, available in the notions section of fabric and quilt shops.

To mark straight lines, use a pencil and a rotary cutting ruler or ¼" masking tape. Apply the tape after the quilt sandwich is layered. Stitch along the edge of the tape. Then remove the tape and reuse it. To prevent a sticky residue, don't leave tape on the quilt top any longer than necessary.

Commercially available quilting designs are available in several formats. Some are stencils that you trace onto the fabric. Others are printed on a paper that can be stitched through and torn away. If your quilt top has a light-colored background, try slipping a printed pattern underneath and tracing the design. A light table will let you do the same with a darker fabric. Of course, you don't have to use a prepared design. With free-motion quilting, you can make up your own design as you go.

The Backing

The backing for the quilt sandwich must be at least 2" larger than the quilt top on each side. For example, if your quilt top measures 36" x 48", you'll need a backing that measures at least 40" x 52". For a large backing, you may have to join several pieces of fabric together. Work out a cutting and piecing plan on paper before you cut into the fabric. To avoid a seam down the middle, cut the backing fabric in half on the crosswise grain, cut one of the pieces in half on the lengthwise grain, and join together as shown. Press the seams open.

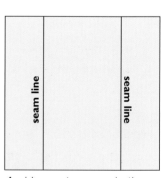

Avoid a center seam in the backing

Bed sheets are another option for quilt backing. Since they have a high thread count, they are difficult to hand-quilt, but easy to quilt by machine. Flannel backings can help baby and juvenile quilts stay put on the bed. For a fun look, or to economize, piece the backing from leftover fabrics or blocks in your collection.

Layering

Place the backing wrong side up on a hard, flat surface, such as a large table or the floor. Tape down the middle of each edge to the surface with $5/8$"-wide masking tape, keeping the fabric taut. Tape out to each corner, keeping the fabric taut and the corners square. Lay the batting on top of the backing and pat out any wrinkles. Center the quilt top on the batting, right side up. Make sure the quilt top looks straight on each side. You can always pat a little extra fullness toward the middle of the quilt top.

I recommend basting with safety pins, particularly for machine quilting. Start at the center of the quilt and insert a pin every three to four inches, working out to the edges. Continue until the entire quilt sandwich is pinned.

To baste with thread, use a large embroidery needle and a single thread knotted at one end. Baste from the center out to the edges in all directions, creating a radiating pattern. Another method is to baste in a grid, spacing the sewing lines three to four inches apart.

Machine Quilting

Most of the quilts in this book are machine-quilted. When you layer your quilt, make up a smaller layered sandwich for practice quilting. Remove the regular presser foot and attach a walking foot or even-feed foot to your machine. There are three layers to be fed through the machine, and the top layer can easily drag. The walking foot feeds all three layers to the needle evenly. Thread the machine with either monofilament or colored cotton thread. Thread the bobbin with cotton thread to match the back of the quilt. Do a little quilting on your practice piece to make sure your machine is in good working order and to give yourself a chance to warm up.

Begin your quilting by stitching in-the-ditch, or along a pieced seam. No marking is necessary. Line up the quilt so it can feed straight through the machine. Spread the fabric apart with your fingers, and stitch as close to the seam as possible. Pick the side without the seam allowances underneath, so that you're stitching through just one layer of fabric on the quilt top. When you move your hands away, the fabric relaxes and hides the stitching. In-the-ditch stitching is the perfect way to define blocks and borders, and it stabilizes the entire quilt in the process. Remove the safety pins as you finish quilting each area.

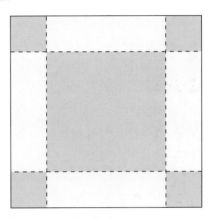

Stitching in-the-ditch

To keep the stitching neat, backtack two stitches at the beginning and end of each run, and clip off the loose threads as you go. After you've quilted in-the-ditch, add more decorative designs in the open spaces. I prefer marking these designs just before I'm going to quilt them, so that they don't rub off while I'm stitching other areas.

> ### ▨ QUILTER'S TIP
>
> *Set up your machine on a large table or use a card table to extend your work surface. As the quilt feeds through the machine, let the excess weight rest on the table instead of dragging over the edge. Roll the edge of a large quilt so that you can maneuver it under the sewing machine arm.*

Free-Motion Quilting

Free-motion quilting is machine quilting that is done over the whole surface of the quilt or within larger spaces. For this quilting, you will need a machine embroidery foot. I like a clear plastic foot that lets me see through to the quilt surface.

Lower the feed dogs so that they are no longer pushing the fabric along their one-way stitching path. The quilt must be free to move from side to side and up and down. Warm up on a practice piece, moving the quilt in different directions under the needle to create random designs or a simple shape, such as a leaf. I admit I was too intimidated to try free-motion quilting until my daughter, Valori, tried it and encouraged me. Rather than stitch without any guidance, I like to make a paper tracing. I might put the tracing paper over a snapshot of a leaf and trace the simple lines, trying for a continuous line design. Tracing helps me get familiar with the pattern, making it easier to quilt. I pin the tracing to the quilt, stitch right over it, and then tear the tracing away. You could also mark the design directly on the quilt surface with marking pencils.

Continous Line Designs for Free-Motion Quilting

Hand Quilting

In traditional hand quilting, straight stitching lines are worked $1/4$" from the seam lines and special designs and motifs fill in the larger spaces. The finer the needle and the thinner the batting, the smaller the stitch. When you first start out, strive for a consistent stitch size rather than tiny stitches. As you practice and do more quilting, your stitches will become both smaller and more consistent.

Most people find it helpful to secure the quilt in a hoop. The three layers are held taut, which makes it easier to get consistent stitches. Traditional hoops are round, but other options include PVC pipe square frames, which give you access to the corners, and a half hoop that lets you quilt right up to the edge. Floor frames are still used for large quilts, but many of today's homes do not have room to leave a frame set up for any length of time.

The actual quilting stitch is done with a short, sharp needle called a "between." Thread the needle with an 18" length of thread and knot the end. Take a stitch through the quilt top only, passing the needle between the fabric threads. Pull gently until the knot opens the weave of the fabric and pops through, lodging itself inside the quilt sandwich.

The stitch uses an up-and-down motion. Use your thimble to push the needle through the quilt top to the back side and then back to the front again, making a stitch no more than $1/8$" long. As you get the feel of it, you will be able to get several stitches on the needle. It takes me about fifteen minutes to get into the rhythm of hand quilting each time I pick it up. When you're near the end of the thread, make a single knot, take a small stitch through the top layer only, and pull the knot through the fabric. Trim off the excess thread and remove the basting.

Binding the Edges

Binding the edges is the final step in making a quilt. Follow these instructions for each quilt in this book.

1 Cut the binding fabric into 1½"-wide strips. Sew the strips together on the diagonal (see page 43) to make one long strip.

2 Measure one edge of the quilt top and add 1". Cut a binding strip this length from the long strip made in step 1. Repeat for each edge of the quilt.

3 Place one side binding strip on the quilt top, right sides together and raw edges aligned, so that the binding extends ½" beyond the quilt top at each end. Use a walking foot to stitch ¼" from the raw edges through all layers. Trim off the excess batting and backing fabric to match the ¼" seam allowance.

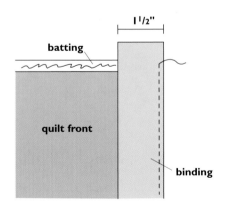

4 Press the long raw edge of the binding strip ¼" to the wrong side. Fold the binding onto the back of the quilt, line up the pressed fold on the stitching line, and pin every few inches. Slip-stitch the binding to the quilt. The thickness of the batting will fill out the binding.

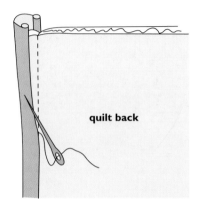

quilt back

5 Repeat steps 3 and 4 to bind the opposite edge of the quilt. Trim both side bindings even with the quilt top. Then bind the remaining two edges, folding in the excess at each end. The binding will overlap at the corners.

fold in ends

A Bound Corner

⊞ SIGNING YOUR QUILT

Sign and date your quilt on the back to document its origin. If you made the quilt for a special person or occasion, add that information along with a personal message. You can make a label out of light-colored fabric and write on it with a permanent pen, or you can embroider or cross-stitch a label. Sometimes, I choose a quilt block that didn't fit on the front of the quilt, write on it, and put it on the back.

CHAPTER 2

Strip Piecing

S trips are the starting point for many quilt blocks. Get comfortable cutting and sewing strips, and you'll have mastered the first lesson any quilter needs to know.

NINE-PATCH

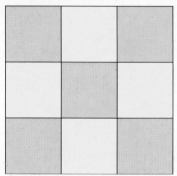

Block Diagram

The Nine-Patch is one of the most basic block constructions in patchwork quilting. It consists of nine squares arranged in three rows to make a larger square. The individual squares can be cut from assorted fabrics or from two colors, for a checkerboard look.

FOR A 6" CHECKERBOARD BLOCK, CUT:

five dark $2^{1}/_{2}$" squares

four light $2^{1}/_{2}$" squares

1. Lay out the squares in three rows of three squares each, alternating the colors.

2. Stitch the squares together in rows. Press the seam allowances toward the darker fabric.

3. Layer row 1 and row 2 right sides together. Because the seams are pressed in opposite directions, they will nest together easily and lock into place. Stitch along one long edge to join the rows. Then join row 3 to row 2. Press both seams in one direction.

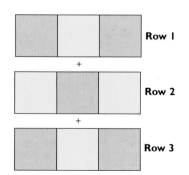

Row 1

+

Row 2

+

Row 3

FOR MULTIPLE BLOCKS, speed up the assembly process by strip-piecing. To practice this technique, cut three $2^{1}/_{2}$" x 42" dark strips and two $2^{1}/_{2}$" x 42" light strips.

1. Layer one dark strip and one light strip right sides together. Stitch together on one long edge, using a $^{1}/_{4}$" seam allowance. Press the seam allowance toward the darker strip. Stitch a second dark strip to the opposite edge of the light strip. Press toward the darker strip.

2. Cut each remaining dark and light strip in half. Stitch one dark and two light strips together. Press toward the darker fabric. (The remaining dark strip is not needed.)

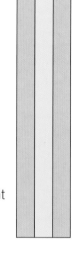

3. You now have two pieced sets. The dark/light/dark set is twice as long as the light/dark/light set. Cut each set into $2^{1}/_{2}$" segments, or the width of a single strip before sewing.

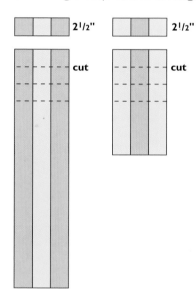

4. Lay out two dark/light/dark segments and one light/dark/light segment in rows, as you did for a single block. Sew the rows together and press. You will have enough segments to make eight 6" blocks.

LOG CABIN

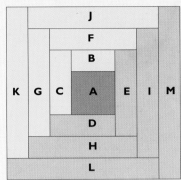

Block Diagram

The Log Cabin block is constructed by sewing strips around a center square and building out in a spiral pattern until the desired block size is reached. The center square (A) is traditionally red, to represent the hearth, and the strips (B, C, D, E, etc.) are the logs. When the strips are cut from two contrasting color families, a zigzag line forms from corner to corner across the block. These diagonal zigzags can create many interesting patterns across the surface of a quilt, depending on how the blocks are arranged.

FOR A 12" BLOCK, CUT:

one $3^1/2$" square (A)

two light strips, 2" x $3^1/2$" (B) and 2" x 5" (C)

two dark strips, 2" x 5" (D) and 2" x $6^1/2$" (E)

two light strips, 2" x $6^1/2$" (F) and 2" x 8" (G)

two dark strips, 2" x 8" (H) and 2" x $9^1/2$" (I)

two light strips, 2" x $9^1/2$" (J) and 2" x 11" (K)

two dark strips, 2" x 11" (L) and 2" x $12^1/2$" (M)

FOR A 6" BLOCK, CUT:

one 2" square (A)

two light strips, $1^1/4$" x 2" (B) and $1^1/4$" x $2^3/4$" (C)

two dark strips, $1^1/4$" x $2^3/4$" (D) and $1^1/4$" x $3^1/2$" (E)

two light strips, $1^1/4$" x $3^1/2$" (F) and $1^1/4$" x $4^1/4$" (G)

two dark strips, $1^1/4$" x $4^1/4$" (H) and $1^1/4$" x 5" (I)

two light strips, $1^1/4$" x 5" (J) and $1^1/4$" x $5^3/4$" (K)

two dark strips, $1^1/4$" x $5^3/4$" (L) and $1^1/4$" x $6^1/2$" (M)

1. Layer square A and strip B right sides together, with B on top. Stitch along one edge, using a $1/4$" seam allowance. Press the seam allowance toward B.

2. Layer AB and C right sides together, with AB on top. Feed the layers through the sewing machine so that B is stitched before A. Press toward C.

3. Layer ABC and D right sides together, with ABC on top. Feed through the sewing machine so that C is stitched before A. Press toward D.

4. Layer ABCD and E right sides together, with ABCD on top. Feed through the sewing machine so that D is stitched first. Press toward E.

5. The first round is now complete. Turn the unit right side up. Note how B, C, D, and E run counterclockwise around A. The next strip, F, will be stitched to the EBC edge. To maintain the proper sequence, always layer the pieces with the existing work on top and feed the previously stitched strip through the machine first. Press the seam allowances toward the outside edge of the block. As the block grows larger, the light/dark diagonal pattern will become more apparent and will alert you as to which color strip to pick up next.

✦ QUILTER'S TIP

Use chain sewing to speed the assembly of multiple Log Cabin blocks. First, stitch all the A's and B's together in an unbroken chain. Clip apart and press. Then chain-sew all the AB units to the C's. Clip apart and press. Continue adding the strips in sequence until all the blocks are completed. If you are using several different fabrics, try to vary the combinations from block to block.

Harmony

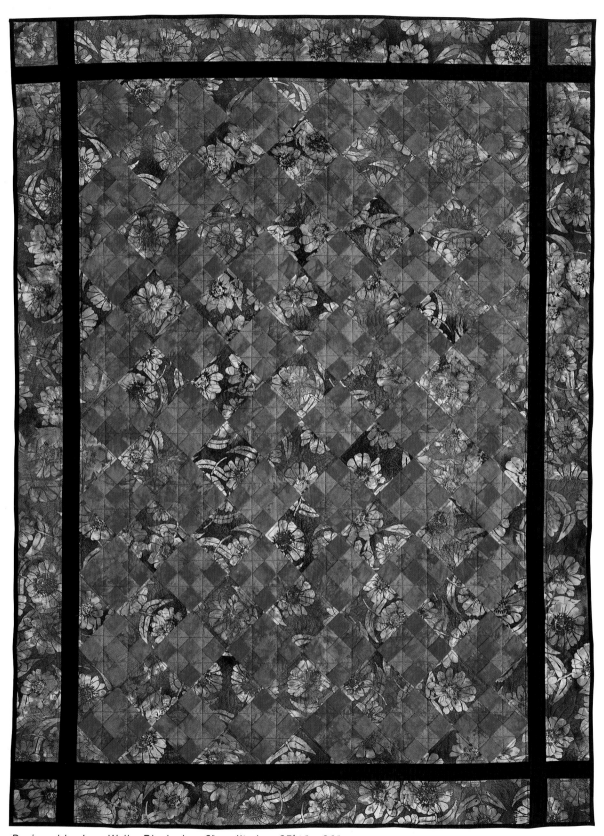

Designed by Jean Wells. Block size, 6"; quilt size, 65 1/2" x 91".

A large-scale batik print was chosen as the theme fabric for this quilt. When you use similar fabrics for the companion block and part of the Nine-Patch squares, crisscrossing paths appear along the quilt surface. In a bright color palette, black lends a defining note.

BASIC INSTRUCTIONS

Nine-Patch Block (page 52)
Diagonal Set (page 44)
Finishing a Quilt (page 46)

MATERIALS

$3^1/_8$ yards pink/turquoise batik
$1^3/_8$ yards dark pink textured solid
$1^1/_8$ yards turquoise textured solid
$^2/_3$ yard black
$^1/_2$ yard for binding
$5^1/_2$ yards backing
70" x 95" batting

CUTTING

Nine-Patch Blocks (54)

From the dark pink textured solid, cut eighteen $2^1/_2$" x 42" strips (A).
From the turquoise textured solid, cut fifteen $2^1/_2$" x 42" strips (B).

Companion Blocks (40)

From the pink/turquoise batik, cut seven $6^1/_2$" x 42" strips. Cut into forty $6^1/_2$" squares.

Setting Triangles

From the pink/turquoise batik, cut two $9^3/_4$" x 42" strips. Cut into seven $9^3/_4$" squares; cut diagonally in both directions for 26 setting triangles (two are discarded). From the leftover fabric strip, cut two $5^1/_8$" squares; cut diagonally in half for four corner setting triangles.

Borders

From the black, cut eight $2^1/_2$" x 42" strips. Sew into one long strip. Cut into two $2^1/_2$" x 77" strips for the side inner borders, two $2^1/_2$" x $55^1/_2$" strips for the top and bottom inner borders, and eight $2^1/_2$" x $5^1/_2$" rectangles (C). From the pink/turquoise batik, cut eight $5^1/_2$" x 42" strips. Sew into one long strip. Cut into two $5^1/_2$" x 77" strips for the side outer borders, two $5^1/_2$" x $51^1/_2$" strips for the top and bottom outer borders, and four $5^1/_2$" squares for the outer border corners (D).

ASSEMBLY

1. Sew the dark pink and turquoise strips together in groups of three, making 7 ABA sets and 4 BAB sets. Cut each set into $2^1/_2$" segments. Join the segments to make 54 Nine-Patch blocks.

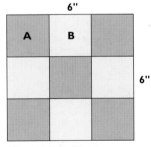

Nine-Patch Block
Make 54

2. Lay out the Nine-Patch blocks and companion blocks on point, as shown in the quilt photograph and quilt diagram (page 56). Place the setting triangles around the edges. Stitch the blocks and setting triangles together in diagonal rows. Press. Join the rows together. Press. Add the corner triangles. Press.

3. Sew the side inner borders to the quilt top. Press. Add the top and bottom inner borders. Press.

4. Stitch C rectangles to the ends of each side outer border, as shown in the border diagram. Press toward the darker fabric. Stitch the remaining C rectangles and the D corner squares to the top and bottom outer borders. Press after each addition. Sew the side outer borders to the quilt top. Press. Add the top and bottom outer borders. Press.

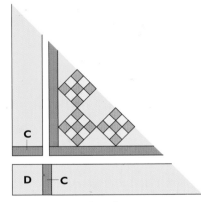

Border Corner Detail

5. Layer and finish the quilt. In *Harmony*, diagonal stitching crisscrosses the blue blocks in each Nine-Patch. The companion block is outlined $^1/_4$" from the edge, and a flowerlike pattern (page 56) is quilted inside. Use a semicircle version of the flower along the border.

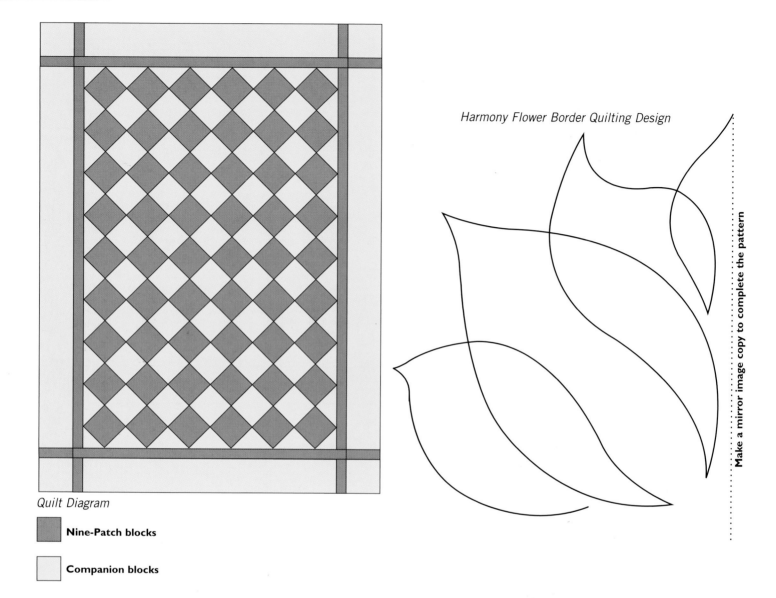

Quilt Diagram

Nine-Patch blocks

Companion blocks

Harmony Flower Border Quilting Design

Make a mirror image copy to complete the pattern

Harmony Flower Quilting Design

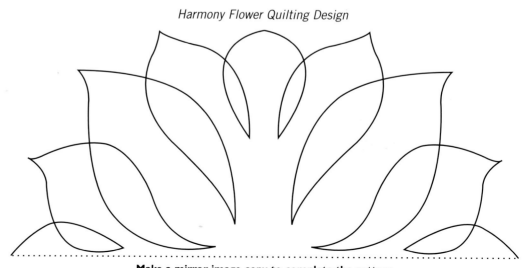

Make a mirror image copy to complete the pattern

Springtime Meadow

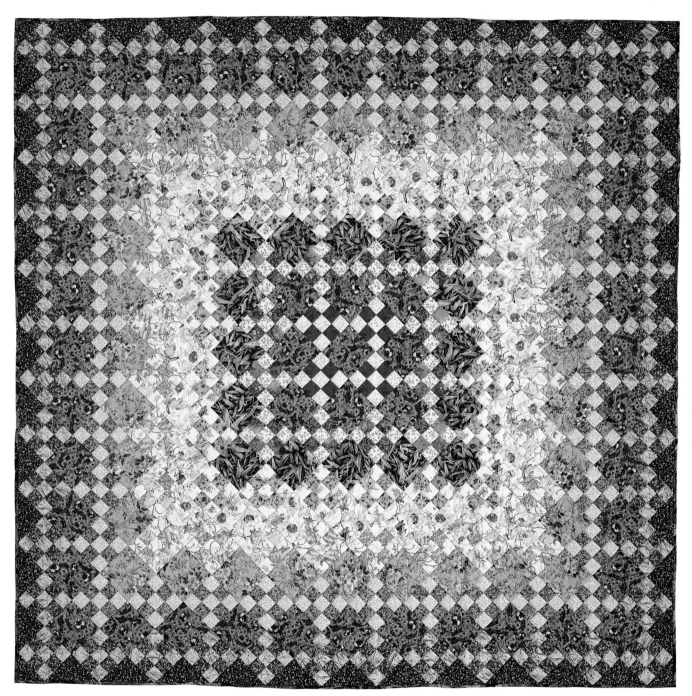

Designed by Jean Wells; inspired by Andrea Balosky. Block size, 4$^{1}/_{2}$"; quilt size, 77" x 77".

This Nine-Patch quilt is a showcase for floral fabrics. Some of the prints are small and packed together, while others are medium or large in scale. In each Nine-Patch, the lighter value is located at the center and the corners, for an overall illusion of looking through a trellis. Although the quilt reads as cream and green, some of the prints have pink and purple flowers.

BASIC INSTRUCTIONS

Nine-Patch Block (page 52)
Diagonal Set (page 44)
Finishing a Quilt (page 46)

MATERIALS

Small green prints:

1³/₈ yards total assorted medium-lights

1¹/₂ yards total assorted medium-darks

1¹/₂ yards total assorted lights

Large green prints:

1¹/₂ yards total assorted medium-darks

¹/₂ yard total assorted medium-lights

⁵/₈ yard total assorted mediums

³/₄ yard dark green print

Scrap (6" x 12") of burgundy

¹/₂ yard for binding

4⁵/₈ yards backing

81" x 81" batting

CUTTING

Nine-Patch Blocks (144)

Use the small green prints and the burgundy.

From the medium-lights, cut twenty-two 2" x 42" strips (A).

From the medium-darks, cut twenty-four 2" x 42" strips (B).

From the burgundy, cut sixteen 2" squares for B.

From the lights, cut twenty-four 2" x 42" strips (C). Cut one strip into twenty 2" squares

Companion Blocks (121)

Use the large green prints.

From the medium-dark, cut nine 5" x 42" strips. Cut into sixty-five 5" squares (D).

From the medium-light, cut three 5" x 42" strips. Cut into twenty-four 5" squares (E).

From the medium, cut four 5" x 42" strips. Cut into thirty-two 5" squares (F).

Setting Triangles

From the dark green print, cut three 7⁵/₈" x 42" strips. Cut into eleven 7⁵/₈" squares; cut diagonally in both directions for 44 setting triangles. From the leftover fabric strip, cut two 4¹/₈" squares; cut diagonally in half for four corner setting triangles.

ASSEMBLY

1. Sew the small green print strips together in groups of three, making 23 sets: 6 ABA, 3 BAB, 3 CAC, 2 ACA, 6 CBC, and 3 BCB. Press toward the darker fabric.

2. Cut each set from step 1 into 2" segments. Join the segments to make 144 Nine-Patch blocks: 56 AB blocks, 28 AC blocks, and 56 BC blocks. Also make 4 BC blocks using the burgundy and light green squares. Each block will have five lighter squares and four darker squares.

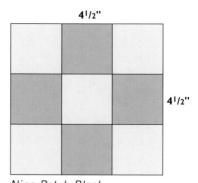

Nine-Patch Block
Make 144 assorted

3. Lay out the Nine-Patch blocks and companion blocks D, E, and F on point, as shown in the quilt photograph (page 57) and quilt diagram. Start at the center of the quilt and work out. Place the setting triangles around the edges.

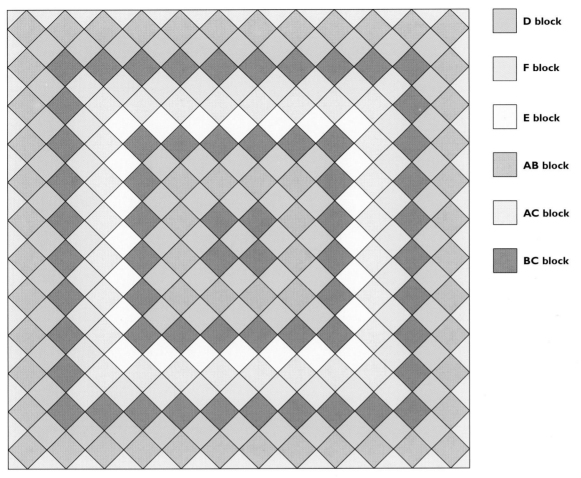

D block

F block

E block

AB block

AC block

BC block

Quilt Diagram

4. Stitch the blocks and setting triangles together in diagonal rows. Press toward the companion blocks and setting triangles. Join the rows together. Press. Add the corner triangles. Press.

5. Layer and finish the quilt. The Nine-Patches in *Springtime Meadow* are stitched in-the-ditch. A petals motif is quilted in the companion blocks.

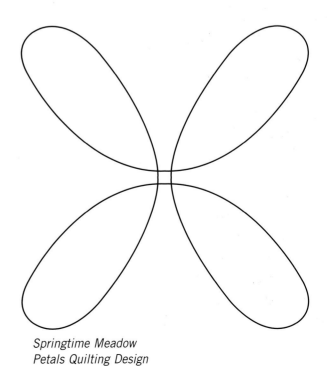

Springtime Meadow
Petals Quilting Design

Indian Summer

Designed by Jean Wells. Block size, 12"; quilt size, 63 1/2" x 87 1/2".

Flannel fabrics give this lap-size Log Cabin quilt a cozy, comfortable feel. Choose three light-value and three dark-value fabrics for the block logs. A dark plaid thrown into the mix spices up the texture. When you lay out the blocks in this straight set, the strong diamond pattern will emerge.

BASIC INSTRUCTIONS

Log Cabin Block (page 53)
Straight Set (page 43)
Finishing a Quilt (page 46)

MATERIALS

1²/₃ yards purple print
³/₄ yard rust print
Darks:
  1 yard purple leaf print
  ³/₄ yard purple/orange plaid
  ¹/₂ yard dark purple
Lights:
  1 yard medium gold print
  ⁵/₈ yard light gold print
  ¹/₂ yard golden tan
¹/₂ yard for binding
5¹/₄ yards backing
68" x 92" batting

CUTTING

Log Cabin Blocks (24)

From the rust print, cut two 3¹/₂" x 42" strips. Cut into twenty-four 3¹/₂" squares (A).

Cut the lights and darks into 2" x 42" strips: 6 golden tan, 7 dark purple, 9 light gold print, 11 purple/orange plaid, 14 medium gold print, and 16 purple leaf print. Cut the strips into smaller pieces, making 24 each of the following:

  2" x 3¹/₂" golden tan (B)
  2" x 5" golden tan (C)
  2" x 5" dark purple (D)
  2" x 6¹/₂" dark purple (E)
  2" x 6¹/₂" light gold print (F)
  2" x 8" light gold print (G)
  2" x 8" purple/orange plaid (H)
  2" x 9¹/₂" purple/orange plaid (I)
  2" x 9¹/₂" medium gold print (J)
  2" x 11" medium gold print (K)
  2" x 11" purple leaf print (L)
  2" x 12¹/₂" purple leaf print (M).

Borders

From the rust print, cut seven 2" x 42" strips. Sew into one long strip. Cut into two 2" x 72¹/₂" strips for the side inner borders and two 2" x 51¹/₂" strips for the top and bottom inner borders.

LOG CABIN KNOW-HOW

The Log Cabin block is sewn from strips that are precut into different lengths. To save time when cutting fabric "logs," stack your 42"-long strips three or four deep and cut the lengths indicated for B, C, D, etc., through the multiple layers. Organize your cut pieces into separate piles and label them with sticky notes. Arrange the piles in the order they will be sewn. Organizing the pieces beforehand will save you time when you sit down to sew.

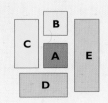

From the purple print, cut eight 6¹/₂" x 42" strips. Sew into one long strip. Cut into two 6¹/₂" x 75¹/₂" strips for the side outer borders and two 6¹/₂" x 63¹/₂" strips for the top and bottom outer borders.

ASSEMBLY

1. Stitch the A's and B's together in pairs, making a continuous chain. Clip apart and press. Chain-sew a C to each AB unit. Clip apart and press. Continue in this manner, adding pieces D through M in sequence, to make 24 Log Cabin blocks. Each block will have a light side and a dark side.

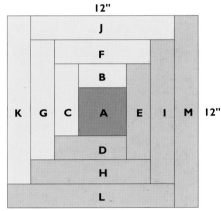

Log Cabin Block
Make 24

2. Lay out the blocks in six rows of four blocks each. Rotate the blocks so that the light and dark areas create a diamond pattern, as shown in the quilt photograph and quilt diagram (page 62).

Quilt Diagram

3. Stitch the blocks together in rows. Press. Join the rows together. Press.

4. Sew the side inner borders to the quilt top. Press. Add the top and bottom inner borders. Press. Add the side outer borders. Press. Add the top and bottom outer borders. Press.

5. Layer and finish the quilt. In *Indian Summer*, the lighter Log Cabin logs are outline-quilted and the darker logs have a pinecone and branch motif. More pine branches are quilted in the outer border.

Indian Summer Pinecone and Branch Quilting Design

Make a mirror image copy to complete the pattern

HAND-TYING A QUILT

Flannel quilts are sometimes tied instead of quilted. Use embroidery floss, lightweight yarn, or heavy cotton thread. Cut a 6" length and thread it through an embroidery needle. Starting from the top of the quilt, push the needle straight down through the layers, and then bring it back up again, emerging one or two fabric threads away. Pull the floss ends snug but not tight, and tie in a square knot. Trim off the excess, leaving $1/2$" tails.

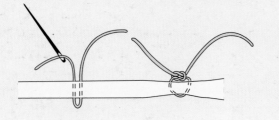

Summer Pines

Designed by Jean Wells and Ursula Searles; tree border inspired by Kathy Sanders. Block size, 11$\frac{1}{4}$"; quilt size, 82$\frac{1}{2}$" x 94$\frac{1}{2}$".

The block arrangement in this quilt suggests pine trees viewed against a summer sky. Notice how bits of red and gold turn up randomly in the print fabrics, like sunlight glistening on a lake. Smaller trees in the border repeat the summer pines theme.

MATERIALS

$4^1/_2$ yards total assorted bright blue prints (including $1^3/_4$ yards for tree border background)

$4^1/_2$ yards total assorted dark green prints

1 yard red print

$1/_8$ yard brown wood-grain print

$1/_2$ yard for binding

$7^3/_8$ yards backing

87" x 99" batting

CUTTING

Log Cabin Blocks (42)

From the red print, cut two $1^3/_4$" x 42" strips. Cut into forty-two $1^3/_4$" squares (A).

From the assorted bright blue prints, cut fifty-five $1^3/_4$" x 42" strips. Mix up the strips for a scrappy look. Cut into smaller pieces, making 42 each of the following:

$1^3/_4$" x $1^3/_4$" (B)
$1^3/_4$" x 3" (C)
$1^3/_4$" x $4^1/_4$" (F)
$1^3/_4$" x $5^1/_2$" (G)
$1^3/_4$" x $6^3/_4$" (J)
$1^3/_4$" x 8" (K)
$1^3/_4$" x $9^1/_4$" (N)
$1^3/_4$" x $10^1/_2$" (O).

From the assorted dark green prints, cut sixty-seven $1^3/_4$" x 42" strips. Mix up the strips for a scrappy look. Cut into smaller pieces, making 42

each of the following:

$1^3/_4$" x 3" (D)
$1^3/_4$" x $4^1/_4$" (E)
$1^3/_4$" x $5^1/_2$" (H)
$1^3/_4$" x $6^3/_4$" (I)
$1^3/_4$" x 8" (L)
$1^3/_4$" x $9^1/_4$" (M)
$1^3/_4$" x $10^1/_2$" (P)
$1^3/_4$" x $11^3/_4$" (Q).

Inner Border

From the red print, cut five $2^3/_4$" x 42" strips. Sew into one long strip. Cut into two $2^3/_4$" x $79^1/_4$" strips for the side inner borders. Cut four $3^1/_8$" x 42" strips. Sew into one long strip. Cut into two $3^1/_8$" x $72^1/_2$" strips for the top and bottom inner borders.

Outer Border

From the assorted dark greens, cut fifteen $2^1/_2$" x 42" strips. Cut into matching sets of rectangles—$2^1/_2$" x $4^1/_2$" (A) and $2^1/_2$" x $6^1/_2$" (B). Make one set per tree, or 52 total.

From the brown wood-grain print, cut two $1^1/_2$" x 42" strips. Cut into fifty-two $1^1/_2$" x $1^1/_4$" rectangles (C) for the tree trunks.

From the blue background fabric, cut seventeen $2^1/_2$" x 42" strips. Cut into two hundred eight $2^1/_2$" squares (D), forty-eight $2^1/_2$" squares (E), and eight $2^1/_2$" x $1^1/_2$" rectangles (F). Cut eight $1^1/_2$" x 42" strips. Cut into forty-eight $1^1/_2$" x

$5^3/_4$" rectangles (G) and eight $1^1/_2$" x $3^1/_8$" rectangles (H). Also cut four $5^1/_2$" squares for the corners.

ASSEMBLY

1. Stitch A and B together in pairs, making a continuous chain. Clip apart and press. Chain-sew a C to each AB unit, placing C on top instead of underneath, so that the strips will circle clockwise as shown. Clip apart and press. Continue in this manner, adding pieces D through Q in sequence, to make 42 Log Cabin blocks. Each block will have a bright blue side and a dark green side.

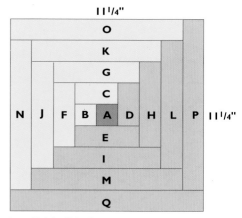

Log Cabin Block
Make 42

2. Lay out the blocks in seven rows of six blocks each. Rotate the blocks to create the pattern shown in the quilt photograph (page 63) and quilt diagram.

3. Stitch the blocks together in rows. Press. Join the rows together. Press.

4. Sew the side inner borders to the quilt top. Press. Add the top and bottom inner borders. Press.

5. Refer to the Flying Geese instructions on page 87. Fold two D squares in half diagonally and finger-press to set the crease. Stitch the D's to an A rectangle and trim as directed. Repeat to make 52 DAD units for the top tier of pine trees for the outer borders. Use the same technique to stitch 2 D's to each B. The 52 DBD units will be wider, to form the pine tree bottom tiers.

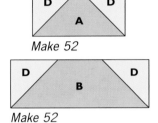

6. Refer to the tree border detail. To assemble row 1 of the side outer border, stitch 14 DAD units and 13 E's together, alternately, making sure all the tree tiers face the same way. Press toward E. Add an F at each end. Press. For row 2, stitch 14 DBD units together. Press in one direction. For row 3, stitch 14 C and 13 G pieces together, alternately, and press toward C. Add an H at each end. Press. Join rows 1, 2, and 3 together to create a border with 14 pine trees. Press toward the base of the trees. Make a second side outer border to match.

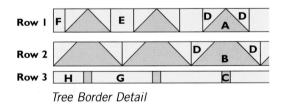

Tree Border Detail

7. Repeat step 6 and use the remaining pieces to assemble the top and bottom outer borders, each with 12 pine trees. Add a $5^1/_2$" square to each end.

8. Sew the side outer borders to the quilt top. Press. Add the top and bottom outer borders. Press.

Quilt Diagram

9. Layer and finish the quilt. In *Summer Pines*, a free-motion leaf pattern is quilted in the Log Cabin blocks. The trees in the border are quilted $1/_4$" from the seam and then echoed in the background fabric. A simple swirl design fills the first border.

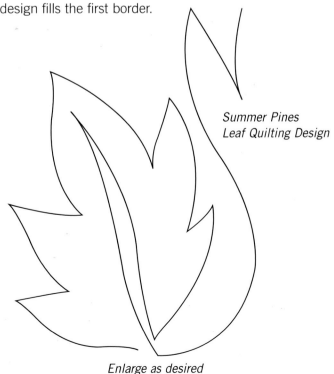

Summer Pines Leaf Quilting Design

Enlarge as desired

Easy Triangles

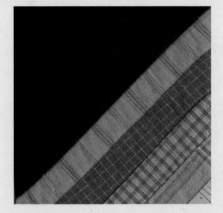

*T*riangles are easy to cut and piece when you start with squares. Contrasting fabrics call attention to the diagonal seam lines where triangles join, making even the simplest blocks appear bold and dramatic.

ROMAN STRIPE

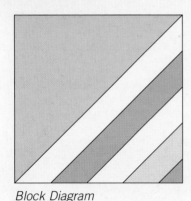

Block Diagram

The Roman Stripe block is made up of two half-square triangles. One triangle is solid and the other is strip-pieced. To make this striped triangle, sew strips of fabric together and then use the solid triangle as a template to cut a matching shape.

FOR A 6" BLOCK, CUT:

one $6^7/8$" square; cut diagonally in half (you'll use one triangle)

five assorted $1^3/8$" x $10^1/2$" strips

---

1. Layer two strips right sides together. Stitch along a $10^1/2$" edge, using a $^1/4$" seam allowance. Press. Add a third strip, and press in the same direction. Repeat until all five strips are joined.

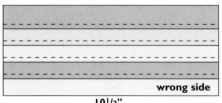

wrong side

$10^1/2$"

2. Lay the five-strip set right side up on your cutting mat. Place the solid triangle on top, right sides together and long edges aligned. Align your cutting ruler on the edge of the triangle and rotary-cut a matching triangle from the strip set. Do not separate the layered pieces; they are ready for sewing.

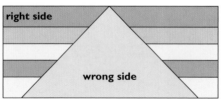

right side

wrong side

3. With the solid triangle on top, stitch the long bias edges together, using a $^1/4$" seam allowance. Be careful not to stretch the bias edges as you handle and sew the pieces.

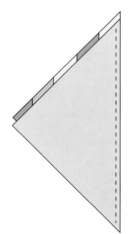

4. Fold the solid triangle over the seam allowance and press from the right side. Trim off the protruding ears to reduce bulk.

PINWHEEL

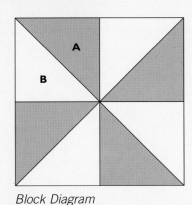

Block Diagram

The Pinwheel block is made up of four half-square triangle units. A two-color arrangement creates the illusion of a pinwheel rotating in the breeze.

FOR A 6" BLOCK, CUT:

two dark $3^7/8$" squares, cut diagonally in half (A)

two light $3^7/8$" squares, cut diagonally in half (B)

---

1. Layer triangles A and B right sides together, with the darker fabric on top. Stitch along the long edge, using a $^1/4$" seam allowance. As you near the end of the seam, pick up another A and B and feed them through the sewing machine without lifting the presser foot. Continue chaining the triangles together.

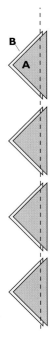

2. Remove the chained pairs from the machine and clip them apart. Press each seam allowance toward the darker fabric. Trim off the ears.

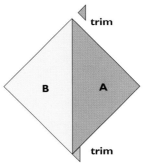

3. Lay out the four AB units right side up as shown, so that the diagonal seams radiate out from the center. To join each pair, turn the right-hand unit facedown on the left-hand unit, nesting the seams. Stitch along the right edge, chaining the units together. Clip apart. Press toward the darker fabric.

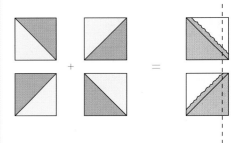

4. Lay out the units right side up as shown, so that the seams radiate out from the center. Turn the right-hand unit facedown on the left-hand unit, and stitch along the right edge. Press the seam allowance in one direction.

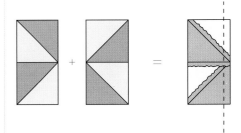

BASIC BLOCK HOURGLASS

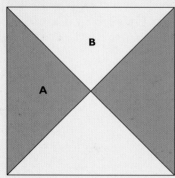

The Hourglass block is made by sewing four quarter-square triangles together. The edges of the triangles form two diagonal lines that intersect at the block center. Use the two-color palette described here to emphasize the hourglass shape, or cut the triangles from multiple fabrics and mix them up for a scrappy look.

Block Diagram

FOR TWO 6" BLOCKS, CUT:

one dark $7^{1}/_{4}$" square, cut diagonally in both directions (A)

one light $7^{1}/_{4}$" square, cut diagonally in both directions (B)

---

1. Layer triangles A and B right sides together, with the darker fabric on top. Stitch along one short edge, using a $^{1}/_{4}$" seam allowance. As you near the end of the seam, pick up another A and B and feed them through the sewing machine without lifting the presser foot. Continue chaining the triangles together.

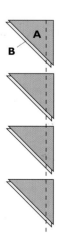

2. Remove the chained pieces from the machine and clip them apart. Press each seam allowance toward the darker fabric.

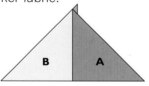

3. Layer two AB units right sides together, butting the seam allowances until you feel the pieces lock. Pin if desired. Stitch along the long edge, chaining until all of the pieces are joined.

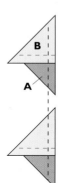

4. Remove the chained pieces from the machine and clip them apart. Press in either direction. Trim off the ears at each corner even with the edge of the block.

⬛ QUILTER'S TIP

To streamline the assembly of multiple half-square triangles, don't cut the triangles individually. Instead, place two cut strips (one of each color) right sides together. Make sure the edges match exactly. Cut through both layers to make the required number of squares and triangles. Do not separate the pieces. Since you started with the fabrics right sides together, the triangles are now ready for sewing. If your cutting mat is extra-large, you can cut your starter strips right sides together too.

Almost Amish

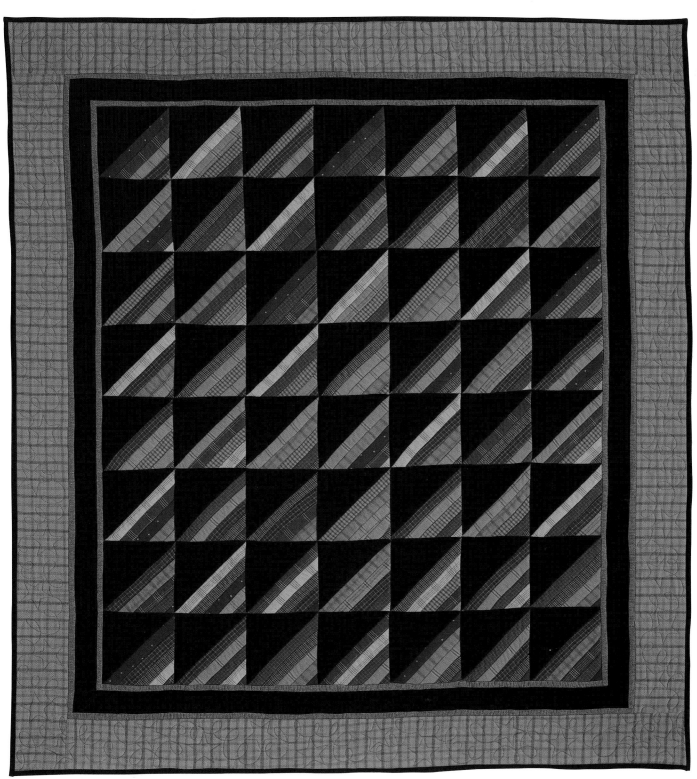

Designed by Jean Wells. Block size, 6"; quilt size, $60\frac{1}{2}$" x $66\frac{1}{2}$".

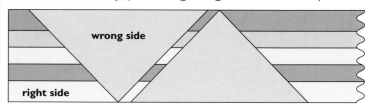

Flannel plaids in fall colors make up the diagonal stripes in this simple, elegant quilt. In the other half of each block, a black triangular "shadow" gives the eye a resting place. The quilt can easily be made larger by adding more blocks.

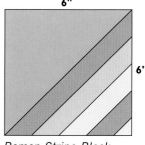

BASIC INSTRUCTIONS

Roman Stripe Block (page 68)
Straight Set (page 43)
Finishing a Quilt (page 46)

MATERIALS

10 fat quarters (18" x 22") in assorted tan, rust, and olive plaids

$1^1/_2$ yards black

$1^3/_8$ yards tan plaid

$3/_8$ yard dull sage green

$3/_8$ yard for binding

$3^2/_3$ yards backing

65" x 71" batting

CUTTING

Roman Stripe Blocks (56)

From each fat quarter, cut ten $1^3/_8$" x 22" strips, or 100 total.

From the black, cut five $6^7/_8$" x 42" strips. Cut into twenty-eight $6^7/_8$" squares; cut diagonally in half for 56 triangles.

Borders

From the black, cut five $2^1/_2$" x 42" strips. Sew into one long strip. Cut into two $2^1/_2$" x $49^1/_2$" strips for the side inner borders and two $2^1/_2$" x $47^1/_2$" strips for the top and bottom inner borders.

From the dull sage green, cut ten 1" x 42" strips. Sew into one long strip. Cut into two 1" x $48^1/_2$" strips (A), two 1" x $43^1/_2$" strips (B), two 1" x $53^1/_2$" strips (C), and two 1" x $48^1/_2$" strips (D) for the inner border accents.

From the tan plaid, cut seven $6^1/_2$" x 42" strips. Sew into one long strip. Cut into two $6^1/_2$" x $54^1/_2$" strips for the side outer borders and two $6^1/_2$" x $60^1/_2$" strips for the top and bottom outer borders.

ASSEMBLY

1. Sew the fat quarter strips together in groups of five, making as many different combinations as possible. Press the seams in one direction. Make 19 strip sets total.

2. Lay one strip set right side up on your cutting mat. Place a black triangle on top, right sides together and long edges parallel. Place a second black triangle next to it, rotating it to avoid waste and also to vary the color pattern. Continue in this way, positioning triangles across the strip set.

3. Align your cutting ruler on top of one black triangle. Using the triangle as a template, rotary-cut a matching triangle from the strip set. Do not separate the layered pieces. Repeat steps 2 and 3 until you have 56 layered pairs total.

4. Stitch the black and striped triangles together as paired along the long edges, chaining until all the pieces are joined. Clip apart. Press toward the black fabric.

Roman Stripe Block
Make 56

5. Lay out the blocks in eight rows of seven blocks each, as shown in the quilt photograph (page 71) and quilt diagram. Stitch the blocks together in rows. Press. Sew the rows together. Press.

6. Sew the A accent strips to the side edges of the quilt. Press toward the outer edge of the quilt. Sew the B accent strips to the top and bottom edges. Press toward the outer edge. Add the side inner borders. Press. Add the top and bottom inner borders. Press. Sew the C accent strips to the side edges. Press. Sew the D accent strips to the top and bottom edges. Press. Add the side outer borders. Press. Add the top and bottom outer borders. Press.

7. Layer and finish the quilt. *Almost Amish* uses outline quilting and other simple quilting lines.

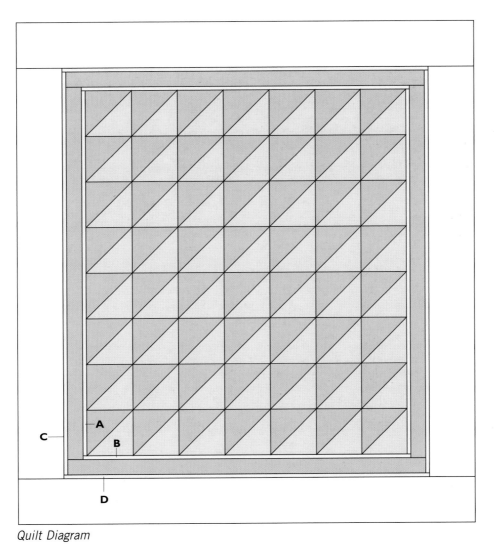

Quilt Diagram

■ **Black solid**

□ **Strip-pieced**

Flying Geese Pinwheels

Designed by Jean Wells. Block size, 6"; quilt size, 88$\frac{1}{2}$" x 112$\frac{1}{2}$".

BASIC INSTRUCTIONS

Pinwheel Block (page 69)
Straight Set (page 43)
Finishing a Quilt (page 46)

Two-color quilts are classic. Red and white solids create lively contrast in this pinwheel quilt and its unusual Flying Geese border, made with half-square triangles. White companion squares make the pinwheels appear more important and give you a place to work some fancy quilting.

MATERIALS

$7^1/_4$ yards white
$4^1/_4$ yards red
$5/_8$ yard for binding
$7^7/_8$ yards backing
93" x 117" batting

CUTTING

Pinwheel Blocks (111)

From the red and the white, cut twenty-three $3^7/_8$" x 42" strips each, or 46 total. Layer the strips right sides together in red/white pairs. Cut into 222 layered $3^7/_8$" squares. Cut diagonally in half for 444 layered triangles (A, B). Do not separate the pairs; they are ready for sewing.

Companion Blocks (110)

From the white, cut nineteen $6^1/_2$" x 42" strips. Cut into one hundred ten $6^1/_2$" squares.

Border

From the red and the white, cut thirteen $2^7/_8$" x 42" strips each, or 26 total. Layer the strips right sides together in red/white pairs. Cut into 180 layered $2^7/_8$" squares. Cut diagonally in half for 360 layered triangles (C, D). Do not separate the pairs; they are ready for sewing.

From the red, cut nine $1^1/_2$" x 42" strips. Sew into one long strip. Cut into two $1^1/_2$" x $102^1/_2$" strips for the side border center bands and two $1^1/_2$" x $78^1/_2$" strips for the top and bottom border center bands.

From the leftover white, cut four $5^1/_2$" squares.

ASSEMBLY

1. Sew the A and B triangles together to make 111 Pinwheel blocks.

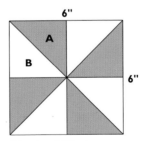

Pinwheel Block
Make 111

2. Lay out the Pinwheel blocks and companion blocks checkerboard-style in 17 rows of 13 blocks each, as shown in the quilt photograph and quilt diagram (page 76). There should be a Pinwheel block in each corner of the layout.

3. Stitch the blocks together in rows. Press. Stitch the rows together. Press.

4. Chain-sew the C and D triangles together in pairs. Clip apart and press.

5. Sew 51 CD units together into one long strip, with all the diagonal seams facing the same direction. Make a second strip to match. Sew two more 51-unit strips with the diagonal seams facing the opposite direction. Make four 39-unit strips, two of them in mirror-image.

6. Sort the eight strips from step 5 into four mirror-image pairs. Sew the two longer pairs to the side border center bands so that the C triangles form the Flying Geese wings. Press toward the center band. Sew the two shorter pairs to the top and bottom border center bands. Press. Add the $5^1/_2$" squares to the ends of the top and bottom borders. Press.

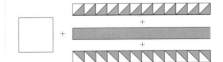

Making the Flying Geese Border

7. Sew the side borders to the quilt so that the geese on the left side of the quilt fly down and the geese on the right side fly up. Press. Add the top and bottom borders to complete the counterclockwise flight path. Press.

8. Layer and finish the quilt. *Flying Geese Pinwheels* is quilted in-the-ditch along all the block, pinwheel, and border seams. A traditional design is machine-quilted in the companion blocks.

Quilt Diagram

✛ THE GRID METHOD FOR HALF-SQUARE TRIANGLES

When you need a large number of matching two-color half-square triangles, try this streamlined grid method developed by Mary Ellen Hopkins. Each square on the grid yields two half-square triangle units. Draw the grid directly on the fabric and sew and cut as directed below. You can also start with a paper grid, which you tear off and discard after the sewing and cutting are complete. Paper tablets with preprinted grids for popular triangle sizes are available at quilt shops.

1. Cut a piece no larger than 18" x 18" from each of your two fabrics. Larger sizes are too hard to maneuver in the sewing machine and still maintain accuracy.

2. Lay the lighter-colored fabric facedown on a flat work surface. Using an ultra-fine permanent pen and a ruler, draw a grid on the fabric surface. Make the grid squares $7/8$" larger than the finished size of a half-square triangle unit. For example, if the finished unit is 2" square, the grid squares should be $2^7/8$".

3. Draw diagonal lines through the grid squares as shown. Draw two dashed lines $1/4$" from each diagonal line. The solid lines are cutting lines. The dashed lines are stitching lines.

Flying Geese Pinwheels
Companion Block Quilting Design

4. Place both pieces of fabric right sides together. Press lightly. Pin in several places. Stitch on all of the dashed lines.

5. Using a rotary cutter and ruler, cut on the solid grid lines and the solid diagonal lines.

6. Open the half-square triangles and press toward the darker fabric. You may need to pick out a couple of threads at the outside points. Trim off the protruding ears.

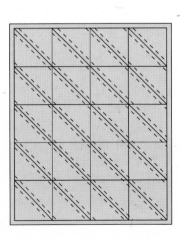

Scrap Basket

Designed by Jean Wells. Block size, 4"; quilt size, 28$\frac{1}{2}$" x 32$\frac{1}{2}$".

An antique quilt in a magazine inspired the hourglass shapes in this scrap quilt. You'll need a wide-ranging assortment of light, medium, and dark values. Be sure to include a strong accent color, such as the red used here. Once you've selected your fabrics, just toss them together. If they look good in a pile, they will look good in the quilt. This is a good way to audition fabrics for a scrap quilt. The hearts are needleturn-appliquéd.

BASIC INSTRUCTIONS

Hourglass Block (page 70)
Hand Appliqué (page 41)
Straight Set (page 43)
Finishing a Quilt (page 46)

MATERIALS

1 yard total assorted red, green, and blue prints
1 yard total assorted off-white prints
$1/4$ yard for binding
1 yard backing
33" x 37" batting
freezer paper

CUTTING

Prepare 18 freezer paper heart templates (page 80).

From the assorted prints, cut 19 red/green/blue and 19 off-white $5^1/4$" squares, or 38 total. Layer the squares right sides together in dark/light pairs. Cut diagonally in both directions for 76 layered triangles (A, B). Do not separate the pairs; they are ready for sewing.

From the off-white prints, cut eighteen $4^1/2$" squares for the heart backgrounds.

From the assorted red and blue prints, cut 18 heart appliqués.

ASSEMBLY

1. Sew the red/green/blue A and off-white B triangles together to make 38 Hourglass blocks.

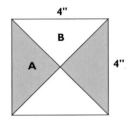

*Hourglass Block
Make 38*

2. Use the freezer paper method to hand-appliqué a heart to each off-white background square.

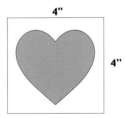

*Appliquéd Heart Block
Make 18*

3. Lay out the pieced and appliquéd blocks in eight rows of seven blocks each. Use any arrangement you like, or follow the quilt photograph and quilt diagram (page 80) for placement. In the project quilt, four Hourglass blocks are grouped together to form a red star, but most of the blocks are rotated at random and face in different directions.

4. Stitch the blocks together in rows. Press. Sew the rows together. Press.

5. Layer and finish the quilt. *Scrap Basket* is machine-quilted in-the-ditch. Outline quilting adds definition to the hearts.

Quilt Diagram

☐ **Heart blocks**

☐ **Hourglass blocks**

Scrap Basket Heart
Template Pattern
Make 18

Woven Tiles

Designed by Jean Wells. Block size, 5"; quilt size, 55$\frac{1}{2}$" x 62$\frac{1}{2}$".

In this variation on the straight set, Hourglass and Four-Patch blocks line up in columns. Dark strips border the columns, highlighting the vertical setting. A large-scale leaf print and extra blocks in the corners help draw the eye around this quilt.

BASIC INSTRUCTIONS

Hourglass Block (page 70)
Straight Set (page 43)
Finishing a Quilt (page 46)

MATERIALS

$1^{1}/_{2}$ yards large dark print
$^{3}/_{4}$ yard dark small print
$^{1}/_{2}$ yard dark medium print
$^{1}/_{2}$ yard light medium print
$^{1}/_{2}$ yard dark textured solid
$^{1}/_{2}$ yard light textured solid
$^{1}/_{2}$ yard for binding
$3^{1}/_{2}$ yards backing
60" x 67" batting

CUTTING

Hourglass Blocks (22)

From the dark medium print and the light textured solid, cut two $6^{1}/_{4}$" x 42" strips each, or four total. Layer the strips right sides together in dark/light pairs. Cut into 11 layered $6^{1}/_{4}$" squares. Cut diagonally in both directions for 44 layered triangles (A, B). Do not separate the pairs; they are ready for sewing.

Four-Patch Blocks (22)

From the dark textured solid and the light medium print, cut four 3" x 42" strips each, or eight total.

Accents, Sashing, and Border

From the dark small print, cut fifteen $1^{1}/_{2}$" x 42" strips. Sew into one long strip. Cut into ten $1^{1}/_{2}$" x 50" strips for the vertical accents and two $1^{1}/_{2}$" x $45^{1}/_{2}$" strips for the horizontal accents.

From the large dark print, *on the lengthwise grain*, cut five $3^{1}/_{2}$" x $50^{1}/_{2}$" strips for the sashing, two $5^{1}/_{2}$" x $52^{1}/_{2}$" strips for the side borders, and two $5^{1}/_{2}$" x $45^{1}/_{2}$" strips for the top and bottom borders.

ASSEMBLY

1. Sew the dark A and light B triangles together to make 22 Hourglass blocks.

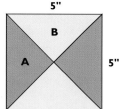

Hourglass Block
Make 22

2. Stitch the 3" x 42" strips together in dark/light pairs. Press. Cut into forty-four 3" segments. Sew the segments together to make 22 Four-Patch blocks.

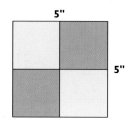

Four-Patch Block
Make 22

3. Lay out the Hourglass blocks and Four-Patch blocks in four columns of ten blocks each, alternating them as shown in the quilt photograph (page 81) and quilt diagram. Stitch the blocks together in columns. Press the seams in one direction.

4. Stitch vertical accent strips to the sides of each column. Press toward the accents. Join the columns together, inserting sashing strips in between and at each side edge. Press. Add a vertical accent strip to each side edge. Press. Add horizontal accent strips to the top and bottom edges. Press.

5. Sew the side borders to the quilt top. Press. Stitch the four remaining patchwork blocks to the ends of the top and bottom borders. Press. Add these borders to the quilt. Press.

6. Layer and finish the quilt. *Woven Tiles* is outline-quilted in the ditch. If you choose a larger print for the border, you can outline the design.

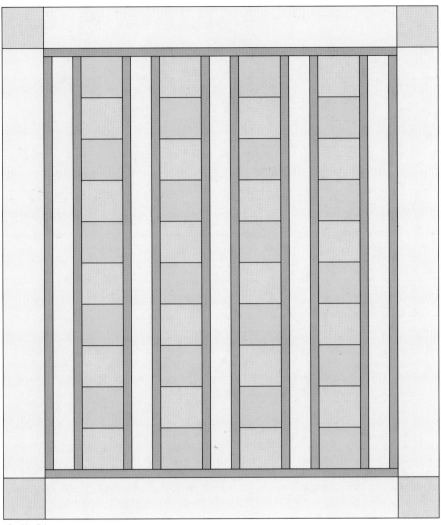

Quilt Diagram

Hourglass blocks

Four-Patch blocks

Stars & Points

*I*f you can piece triangles, then you can make perfect stars with sharp points. Watch how smaller pieces quickly add up to a sparkling whole.

DOLLEY MADISON STAR

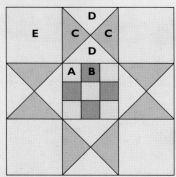

Block Diagram

I n the Dolley Madison Star, four Hourglass units form star points around a little Nine-Patch in the center. In a 12" block, the center unit is 4" square, which means that the nine individual squares are cut one-third that size plus seam allowance, or a bit less than $1^7/_8$". To make this irregular cut, line up your ruler a little before the $1^7/_8$" mark instead of exactly on it.

FOR A 12" BLOCK, CUT:

five scant $1^7/_8$" squares (A)

four scant $1^7/_8$" squares (B)

two dark $5^1/_4$" squares, cut diagonally in both directions (C)

two light $5^1/_4$" squares, cut diagonally in both directions (D)

four light $4^1/_2$" squares (E)

---

1. Sew squares A and B together to make one Nine-Patch unit (see page 52).

Make 1

2. Sew triangles C and D together to make four Hourglass units (see page 70).

Make 4

3. Lay out the pieced units and plain squares in three rows as shown, so that the dark C triangles form the star points. Stitch the units together in rows. Press toward the Hourglass units. Join the rows together, butting the seams. Press.

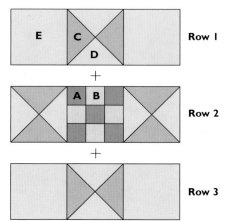

Row 1
+
Row 2
+
Row 3

FLYING GEESE

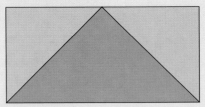

Block Diagram

The Flying Geese unit looks like two half-square triangles joined at the center, except there is no seam. Some sample finished sizes are 6" x 3" and 4" x 2". The unit can be made in several ways. The method given here involves some fabric waste but makes it easy for beginners to sew accurate diagonal seams. For each unit, you'll start with one rectangle and two squares.

FOR A 6" X 3" UNIT, CUT:

one $6^1/2$" x $3^1/2$" rectangle (A)

two $3^1/2$" squares (B)

FOR A 4" X 2" UNIT, CUT:

one $4^1/2$" x $2^1/2$" rectangle (A)

two $2^1/2$" squares (B)

---

1. Fold one B square diagonally in half and press lightly.

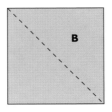 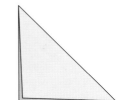

2. Unfold the square. Align it on one end of rectangle A, right sides together. Stitch on the diagonal fold line through both layers.

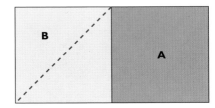

3. Trim off the excess $^1/4$" beyond the stitching line.

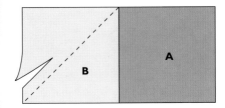

4. Fold the remaining triangular piece over the seam allowance and press from the right side.

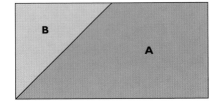

5. Repeat steps 1–3 for the other side of rectangle A.

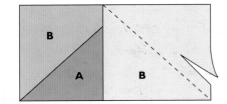

6. Fold back and press the second triangle. The overlapping seams at the top of the unit will disappear into the seam allowance when the unit is joined to other pieces.

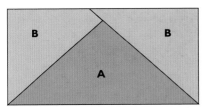

✺ QUILTER'S TIP

Another name for the Flying Geese unit is "double half-square triangles."

SAWTOOTH STAR

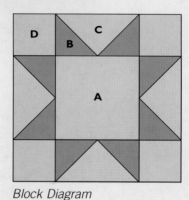

Block Diagram

The Sawtooth Star block uses two basic shapes: the square and the triangle. There are four squares in the corners and a larger square in the center. Look closely at the star points to pick out the Flying Geese units.

FOR A 12" BLOCK, CUT:

one $6^1/2$" square (A)

eight $3^1/2$" squares (B)

four $3^1/2$" x $6^1/2$" rectangles (C)

four $3^1/2$" squares (D)

FOR AN 8" BLOCK, CUT:

one $4^1/2$" square (A)

eight $2^1/2$" squares (B)

four $2^1/2$" x $4^1/2$" rectangles (C)

four $2^1/2$" squares (D)

FOR A 6" BLOCK, CUT:

one $3^1/2$" square (A)

eight 2" squares (B)

four 2" x $3^1/2$" rectangles (C)

four 2" squares (D)

1. Sew pieces B and C together to make four Flying Geese units (see page 87).

Flying Geese Unit
Make 4

2. Lay out pieces A, BC, and D in rows as shown, so that the B triangles form the star points. Stitch the pieces together in rows. Press rows 1 and 3 toward D and row 2 toward A. Join the rows, butting the seams. Press.

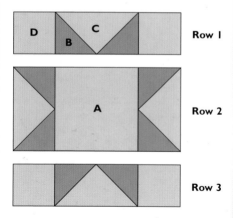

Row 1

Row 2

Row 3

Scottie's Quilt

Designed by Jean Wells. Block size, 12"; quilt size, 61¹/2" x 74¹/2".

A Scottie dog theme print is perfect for a little boy's quilt. Dolley Madison Star blocks in two different fabric combinations keep the eye moving around the quilt. The background and sashing strips are cut from a white cloud fabric to "float" the blocks.

BASIC INSTRUCTIONS

Dolley Madison Star (page 86)
Straight Set (page 43)
Finishing a Quilt (page 46)

MATERIALS

$3^3/4$ yards white cloud print
$1^1/4$ yards blue Scottie theme print
$1^1/4$ yards red print
1 yard blue print
$1/4$ yard black plaid
$1/2$ yard for binding
$3^3/4$ yards backing
66" x 79" batting

CUTTING

Dolley Madison Star Blocks (20)

From the red print, cut four scant $1^7/8$" x 42" strips each. Cut each strip in half, for eight strips total (A).

From the black plaid, cut four scant $1^7/8$" x 42" strips each. Cut each strip in half and discard one for seven strips total (B).

From the blue Scottie theme print, cut two $4^1/2$" x 42" strips. Cut into ten $4^1/2$" squares (center square).

From the red and the blue prints, cut five $5^1/4$" x 42" strips each, or ten total. From the white cloud print, cut ten $5^1/4$" x 42" strips. Layer the strips right sides together in red/white and blue/white pairs. Cut into 40 layered $5^1/4$" squares; cut diagonally in both directions for 160 layered triangles (C, D). Do not separate the pairs; they are ready for sewing.

From the white cloud print, cut ten $4^1/2$" x 42" strips. Cut into eighty $4^1/2$" squares (E).

Sashing

From the white cloud print, cut seventeen $1^1/2$" x 42" strips. Cut into twenty-five $1^1/2$" x $12^1/2$" strips for the vertical sashing. Sew the remaining pieces into one long strip. Cut into six $1^1/2$" x $53^1/2$" strips for the horizontal sashing.

Border

From the blue Scottie theme print, cut seven $4^1/2$" x 42" strips. Sew into one long strip. Cut into two $4^1/2$" x $66^1/2$" strips for the side borders and two $4^1/2$" x $53^1/2$" strips for the top and bottom borders.

ASSEMBLY

1. Sew the red print and black plaid strips together in groups of three, making 3 ABA sets and 2 BAB sets. Cut each set into scant $1^7/8$" segments, until you have 28 ABA segments and 14 BAB segments. Join the segments to make 14 Nine-Patch units. Use your rotary cutter and ruler to true up each unit to $4^1/2$" square (for a 4" finished size).

Make 14

2. Sew the C and D triangles together to make 40 blue/white and 40 red/white Hourglass units.

Make 40   *Make 40*

3. Stitch the Nine-Patch units, blue/white Hourglass units, and 40 E squares together in rows as shown. Join the rows to make ten Dolley Madison Star blocks.

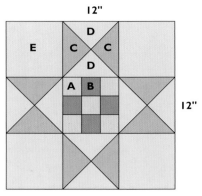

Dolley Madison Star Block
Make 10

4. Stitch the center squares, red/white Hourglass units, and 40 E squares together to make ten Dolley Madison Star Variation blocks.

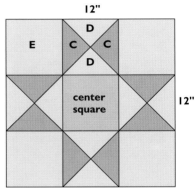

Dolley Madison Star Variation
Make 10

5. Lay out all the Dolley Madison Star blocks in five rows of four blocks each, alternating the colors as shown in the quilt photograph (page 89) and quilt diagram. Stitch the blocks together in rows, inserting vertical sashing strips in between and at each end. Press. Join the rows together, inserting horizontal sashing strips in between and at the top and bottom edges. Press.

6. Add the side borders to the quilt top. Press. Stitch the four remaining Nine-Patches to the ends of the top and bottom borders. Press. Add these borders to the quilt. Press.

7. Layer and finish the quilt. In *Scottie's Quilt*, the star shape is outline-quilted. Free-motion quilting in the background and border mimics the fabric's cloud design.

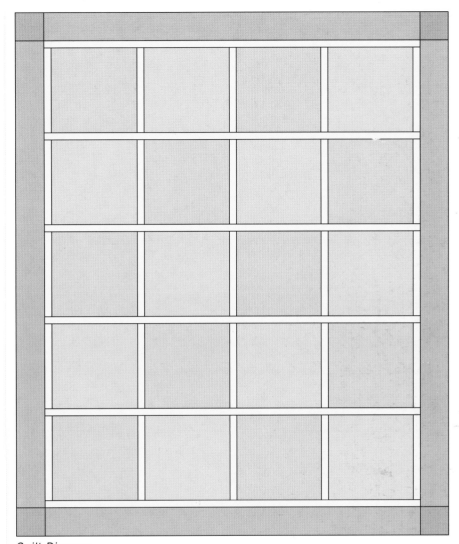

Quilt Diagram

Dolley Madison Star block

Dolley Madison Star Variation

Wings in Motion

Designed by Pat Welsh. Block size, 12"; quilt size, 63¹/₂" x 80¹/₂".

A dragonfly-and-butterfly print inspired the palette for *Wings in Motion*. Large squares set on point offer the perfect spot to show off this attractive print. Flying Geese strips look like sashing at first glance but are actually part of the blocks. In the outer four corners of the quilt, dragonfly appliqués and Flying Geese continue the "wings in motion" theme.

BASIC INSTRUCTIONS

Fusible Appliqué (page 42)
Flying Geese Unit (page 87)
Diagonal Set (page 44)
Finishing a Quilt (page 46)

MATERIALS

2³/₄ yards green theme print
1⁵/₈ yards light sage/beige print
1¹/₄ yards dark olive textured solid
¹/₂ yard each green, purple, and melon prints
¹/₄ yard orange print
¹/₂ yard for binding
4⁷/₈ yards backing
68" x 85" batting
paper-backed fusible web
embroidery floss

CUTTING

Flying Geese Blocks (12)

From the green theme print, cut three 8¹/₂" x 42" strips. Cut into twelve 8¹/₂" squares.

From the green, purple, and melon prints, cut eight 1¹/₂" x 42" strips each. Cut each strip into sixteen 1¹/₂" x 2¹/₂" rectangles, or 384 total.

From the light sage/beige print, cut twenty-eight 1¹/₂" x 42" strips. Cut into 1¹/₂" squares, or 768 total.

From the orange print, cut three 2¹/₂" x 42" strips. Cut into forty-eight 2¹/₂" squares.

Companion Blocks (6)

From the green theme print, cut two 12¹/₂" x 42" strips. Cut into six 12¹/₂" squares.

Setting Triangles

From the dark olive textured solid, cut two 18¹/₄" x 42" strips. Cut into three 18¹/₄" squares; cut diagonally in both directions for ten setting triangles (two are discarded). From the leftover strip, cut two 9³/₈" squares; cut diagonally in half for four corner setting triangles.

Borders

From the light sage/beige print, cut six 1¹/₂" x 42" strips. Sew into one long strip. Cut into two 1¹/₂" x 68¹/₂" strips for the side inner borders and two 1¹/₂" x 53¹/₂" strips for the top and bottom inner borders.

From the green theme print, cut seven 5¹/₂" x 42" strips. Sew into one long strip. Cut into two 5¹/₂" x 70¹/₂" strips for the side outer borders and two 5¹/₂" x 53¹/₂" strips for the top and bottom outer borders.

From the green, purple, and melon prints, cut four 2" x 3¹/₂" rectangles.

From the dark olive, cut two 5¹/₂" squares and eight 2" squares. Also cut one 1¹/₂" x 42" strip. Cut into four 1¹/₂" x 3¹/₂" strips and four 1¹/₂" x 5¹/₂" strips. All of these pieces are for the corner squares.

Select two dragonfly motifs, no larger than 4¹/₂", from the theme fabric. Use fusible web and follow the manufacturer's instructions to make two fusible dragonfly appliqués.

ASSEMBLY

1. Sew two light sage/beige print squares to each green, purple, and melon print rectangle to make 384 Flying Geese units.

Make 384 assorted

2. Stitch the Flying Geese units together in sets of eight, selecting the colors at random. Press in one direction. Make 48 sets total.

Make 48 assorted

3. Sew two Flying Geese strips to opposite edges of six 8¹/₂" theme print squares, so that the geese on the left side fly down and the geese on the right side fly up. Press toward the square. Make six more units, reversing the geese direction.

Make 6

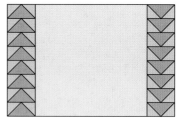

Make 6

4. Sew two 2¹/₂" squares to each remaining Flying Geese strip.

5. Join the units from steps 3 and 4, making six blocks with a clockwise flight path and six blocks with a counter-clockwise flight path.

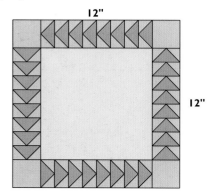

Flying Geese Blocks
Make 12 (reverse 6)

6. Lay out the plain and Flying Geese theme print squares on point, alternating the flight paths, as shown in the quilt photograph (page 92) and quilt diagram. Place the setting triangles around the edges. Stitch the blocks and setting triangles together in diagonal rows. Press. Join the rows. Press. Add the corner triangles. Press.

7. Sew two dark olive 2" squares to each 2" x 3¹/₂" rectangle to make four Flying Geese units. Sew the units together in pairs. Add two 1¹/₂" x 3¹/₂" dark olive strips to the top and bottom edges. Press toward the dark olive strips. Add dark olive 1¹/₂" x 5¹/₂" strips to the two outside edges. Press.

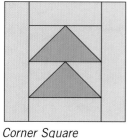

Corner Square
Make 2

8. Fuse a dragonfly appliqué to each 5¹/₂" square. Work buttonhole stitch in contrasting floss around the edges of the appliqué.

9. Sew the side inner borders to the quilt top. Press. Add the top and bottom inner borders. Press. Add the side outer borders. Press. Sew the Flying Geese and appliquéd corner units to the top and bottom outside borders. Press toward the border. Join these borders to the quilt. Press.

10. Layer and finish the quilt. In *Wings in Motion*, the Flying Geese are outline-quilted and a gentle swirl design fills all of the large print squares.

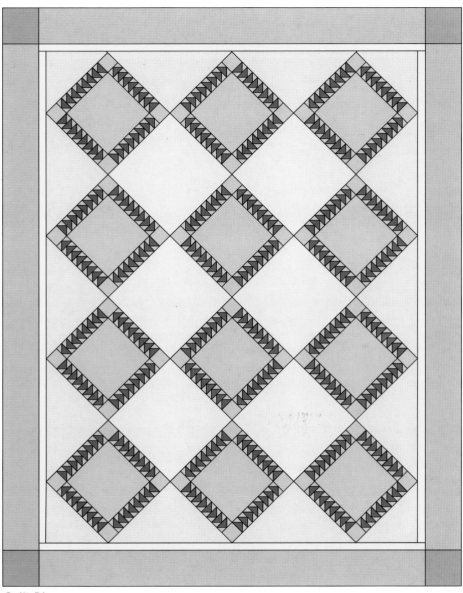

Quilt Diagram

Flying Geese Blocks

Companion Blocks

Designed by Jean Wells. Block size, 12"; quilt size, 82$\frac{1}{2}$" x 82$\frac{1}{2}$".

Sawtooth Stars set on point are the key players in this quilt. A 6" star fits neatly within each 12" block. To create the smaller floating stars, half-square triangles are added to the ends of the sashing strips. The fabrics for this quilt are heirloom prints. Most are monochromatic.

BASIC INSTRUCTIONS

Sawtooth Star Block (page 88)
Diagonal Set (page 44)
Finishing a Quilt (page 46)

MATERIALS

$7^1/4$ yards black
$1/2$ to $5/8$ yard each seven or more
   small prints in assorted colors
$1/2$ yard for binding
$7^3/8$ yards backing
87" x 87" batting

CUTTING

Star Blocks (25)

From a small print, cut one $3^1/2$" x 42" strip and one 2" x 42" strip. Cut into nine $3^1/2$" squares (A, E) and eight 2" squares (B). Repeat until you have enough matching sets for 25 blocks.

From the black, cut fourteen 2" x 42" strips. Cut into one hundred 2" x $3^1/2$" rectangles (C) and one hundred 2" squares (D). Cut twenty-five $3^1/2$" x 42" strips. Cut into one hundred $3^1/2$" x $6^1/2$" rectangles (F) and one hundred $3^1/2$" squares (G).

Sashing

From the black, cut twenty-two $2^1/2$" x 42" strips. Cut into two $2^1/2$" x $16^1/2$" strips (A), twelve $2^1/2$" x $14^1/2$" strips (B), and fifty $2^1/2$" x $12^1/2$" strips (C).

From a small print, cut one $2^1/2$" square (D) for the sashing square/ small star center and eight $1^1/2$"

squares (E) for the small star points. Repeat until you have enough matching sets for 24 small stars.

Setting Triangles

From the black, cut three $21^1/4$" squares; cut diagonally in both directions for 12 setting triangles. Cut two 12" squares; cut diagonally in half for four corner triangles.

ASSEMBLY

1. Stitch two matching B squares to each C rectangle to make 100 Flying Geese units. Join pieces A, BC, and D to make twenty-five 6" Sawtooth Star blocks.

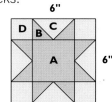

Sawtooth Star Block
Make 25

2. Stitch 2 E squares to each F rectangle to make 100 Flying Geese units. Join the 6" Sawtooth Star blocks and pieces EF and G to make twenty-five 12" Double Sawtooth Star blocks.

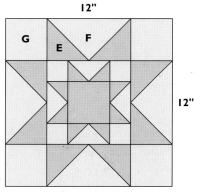

Double Sawtooth Star Block
Make 25

3. Lay out the blocks in diagonal rows. Insert sashing strips A, B, and C, sashing squares D, and the setting triangles as shown in the quilt diagram (page 98). Adjust your arrangement as needed so that the star colors move around the quilt.

4. Stitch two $1^1/2$" squares to the ends of the sashing strips, as if you were making Flying Geese units. Match the colors to the sashing squares. When the sashing strips and squares are joined, these pieces will form small stars.

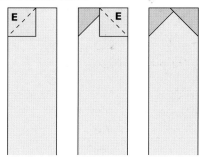

Making the Small Star Points

5. Stitch the blocks, sashing strips, and setting triangles together in diagonal rows. Press toward the sashing. Stitch the remaining sashing strips and sashing squares together. Press. Join the block rows and sashing rows together. Press. Add the corner triangles. Press. Note that the setting triangles are slightly larger than required. Use your rotary cutter and ruler to true up the edges.

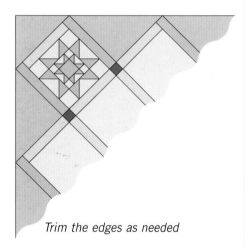

Trim the edges as needed

6. Layer and finish the quilt. The stars in *Primarily Stars* are outline-quilted and then quilted again $1/4$" in from the edge. A simple, traditional quilting design is used in the setting triangles.

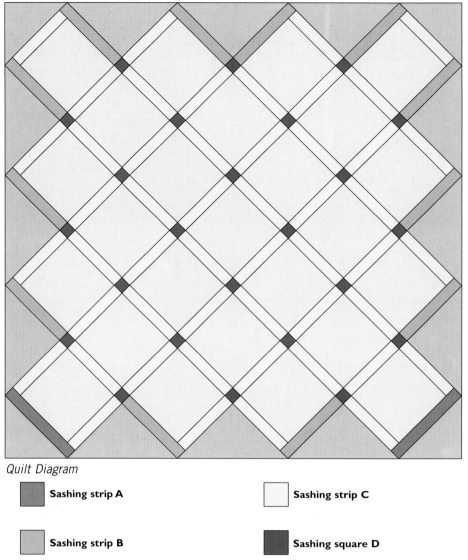

Quilt Diagram

■ **Sashing strip A**	□ **Sashing strip C**
■ **Sashing strip B**	■ **Sashing square D**

Sawtooth Trail

Designed by Ursula Searles. Block size, 8"; quilt size, 76¹/₂" x 92¹/₂".

CHAPTER 5

Combination Blocks

Create different block personalities with units you already know how to piece. Playing with the sizes or rotating a unit on point is all it takes to get a totally new look.

DOUBLE DUTCH

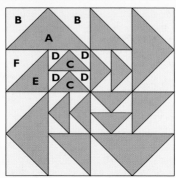

Block Diagram

Although the Double Dutch block looks complex, it is actually made up of just two units—Flying Geese (in two sizes) and half-square triangles. To create the illusion of a whirling windmill, use a darker color for the half-square triangles and the smaller Flying Geese units in the middle.

FOR A 12" BLOCK, CUT:

four $6^1/2$" x $3^1/2$" rectangles (A)

eight $3^1/2$" squares (B)

eight $3^1/2$" x 2" rectangles (C)

sixteen 2" squares (D)

two $3^7/8$" squares, cut diagonally in half (E)

two $3^7/8$" squares, cut diagonally in half (F)

1. Stitch 2 B's to each A to make four large Flying Geese units. Use the piecing method on page 87.

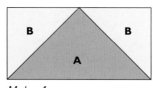

Make 4

2. Stitch 2 D's to each C to make eight small Flying Geese units. Sew the small units together in pairs.

Make 4

3. Stitch E and F together in pairs to make four half-square triangle units.

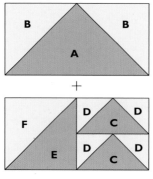

Make 4

4. Sew a half-square triangle unit and a small Flying Geese unit together as shown. Press toward E. Join a large Flying Geese unit to the top edge. Press toward A. Make four units total.

Make 4

5. Lay out the four units from step 4 as shown. Sew the units together in pairs, pressing the seams in opposite directions. Join the pairs together, butting the seams. Press.

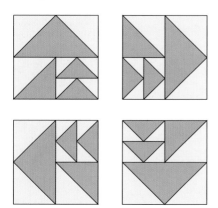

Assembling the Block

NINE-PATCH-IN-A-SQUARE

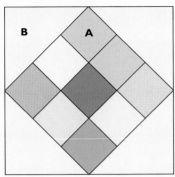

Block Diagram

When you sew a Nine-Patch from a variety of fabrics, instead of two, it takes on a scrappy look. Turning the Nine-Patch on point adds even more interest. Triangles fill in the corners to make the block square again.

FOR A 6" BLOCK, CUT:

nine assorted $1^7/8$" squares (A)

two 4" squares, cut diagonally in half (B)

1. Lay out the A squares in three rows, adjusting until you have an arrangement you like.

2. Sew the squares together in rows. Press the seams in rows 1 and 3 toward the outside edge and the seams in row 2 toward the middle. Stitch row 1 to row 2, butting the seams. Press. Stitch row 3 to row 2. Press.

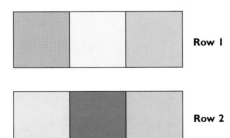

Row 1

Row 2

Row 3

Make a Nine-Patch

3. Stitch two B triangles to opposite edges of the Nine-Patch, being careful not to stretch the bias edges. Press toward B. Stitch B triangles to the remaining two edges. The triangle seams should overlap slightly at the corners of the Nine-Patch. Press.

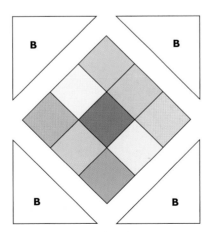

Add the corner triangles

4. Use your rotary cutter and ruler to true up the block to $6^1/2$" square (for a 6" finished size).

AUNT VINA'S FAVORITE

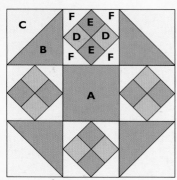

Block Diagram

Aunt Vina's Favorite combines half-square triangles and Four-Patches turned on point. Put together, these units create a circular path around the square in the center.

FOR A 12" BLOCK, CUT:

one $4^1/_2$" square (A)

two dark $4^7/_8$" squares, cut diagonally in half (B)

two light $4^7/_8$" squares, cut diagonally in half (C)

eight medium $1^7/_8$" squares (D)

eight dark $1^7/_8$" squares (E)

eight light $2^7/_8$" squares, cut diagonally in half (F)

1. Stitch the B and C triangles together in pairs. Press toward the darker fabric.

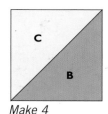

Make 4

2. Stitch the D and E squares together in pairs. Press toward the darker fabric. Stitch the DE units together in pairs to make four Four-Patch units. Press.

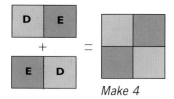

Make 4

3. Stitch 2 F triangles to opposite edges of each Four-Patch. Press toward F. Stitch 2 F triangles to the remaining edges. Press.

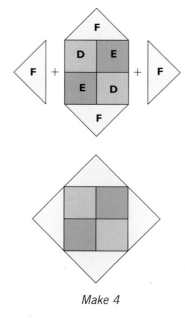

Make 4

4. Lay out the nine units in three rows as shown. Stitch together in rows. Press toward B in rows 1 and 3 and toward A in row 2. Join the rows together. Press.

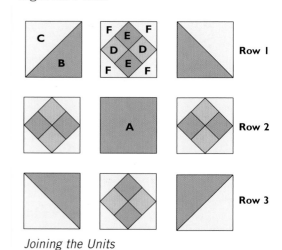

Joining the Units

Summer Fun

Designed by Jean Wells. Block size, 12"; quilt size, 48¹/₂" x 61¹/₂".

T he Double Dutch block generates a lot of movement when you introduce a secondary color pattern. I chose deep blue to accentuate the inner pinwheels and to heighten the illusion of spinning. A batik fabric in summery blues and greens inspired the palette.

BASIC INSTRUCTIONS

Double Dutch Block (page 104)
Straight Set (page 43)
Finishing a Quilt (page 46)

MATERIALS

$2^1/8$ yards yellow batik
$1^2/3$ yards green/yellow/blue batik
$1^1/8$ yards green batik
1 yard blue batik
$3/8$ yard for binding
3 yards backing
53" x 66" batting

CUTTING

Double Dutch Blocks (12)

From the green/yellow/blue batik, cut eight $3^1/2$" x 42" strips. Cut into forty-eight $3^1/2$" x $6^1/2$" rectangles (A).

From the yellow batik, cut eight $3^1/2$" x 42" strips. Cut into ninety-six $3^1/2$" squares (B). Cut ten 2" x 42" strips. Cut into one hundred ninety-two 2" squares (D). Cut three $3^7/8$" x 42" strips. Cut into twenty-four $3^7/8$" squares; cut diagonally in half (F).

From the blue and the green batiks, cut eight 2" x 42" strips each. Cut into ninety-six 2" x $3^1/2$" rectangles for each fabric, or 192 total (C).

From the blue batik, cut three $3^7/8$" x 42" strips. Cut into twenty-four $3^7/8$" squares; cut diagonally in half (E).

Sashing, Inner Border

From the green batik, cut eleven $1^1/2$" x 42" strips. Cut into eight $1^1/2$" x $12^1/2$" strips for the vertical sashing and five $1^1/2$" x $38^1/2$" strips for the

horizontal sashing and the top and bottom inner borders. Sew the remaining pieces into one long strip. Cut into two $1^1/2$" x $53^1/2$" strips for the side inner borders.

Outer Border

From the green/yellow/blue batik, cut six $4^1/2$" x 42" strips. Sew together into one long strip. Cut into two $4^1/2$" x $53^1/2$" strips for the side outer borders and two $4^1/2$" x $48^1/2$" strips for the top and bottom outer borders.

ASSEMBLY

1. Stitch 2 B's to each A to make 48 large Flying Geese units. Stitch 2 D's to each C to make 96 small Flying Geese units. Stitch the E's and F's together in pairs to make 48 half-square triangle units.

2. Stitch the small Flying Geese units together in contrasting pairs, with the color you've chosen for the inner pinwheel on the bottom (blue in the featured quilt).

Make 48

3. Join the large and small Flying Geese units and the EF half-square triangle units to make 12 Double Dutch blocks.

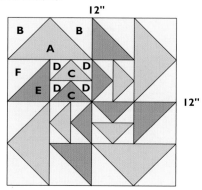

*Double Dutch Block
Make 12*

4. Lay out the blocks in four rows of three blocks each, as shown in the quilt photograph (page 107) and quilt diagram. Stitch the blocks together in rows, inserting vertical sashing strips in between. Press toward the sashing. Join the rows, inserting horizontal sashing strips in between. Press.

5. Sew the top and bottom inner borders to the quilt top. Press toward the borders. Add the side inner borders. Press. Add the side outer borders. Press. Add the top and bottom outer borders. Press.

6. Layer and finish the quilt. The patchwork shapes in *Summer Fun* are outline-quilted, and a sun motif is quilted in the border. This quilt just had a sunny feeling.

Quilt Diagram

Summer Fun
Sun Quilting Design

COMBINATION BLOCKS **109**

Nostalgic Nine-Patch

Designed by Jean Wells. Block size, 6"; quilt size, 46¹/₂" x 46¹/₂".

Vintage-style textiles went into this allover Nine-Patch design. The various colors and textures are arranged in a random pattern that keeps the eye moving over the surface of the quilt. A red bandana print creates a soft stripe around the edges, enhancing the mitered border's framing effect.

BASIC INSTRUCTIONS

Nine-Patch-in-a-Square Block (page 105)
Straight Set (page 43)
Mitered Corner Borders (page 45)
Finishing a Quilt (page 46)

MATERIALS

$2/3$ yard dark print
$2/3$ yard light print
$1^1/2$ yards red bandana stripe print
$1/4$ yard each nine assorted small prints
$3/8$ yard for binding
$2^7/8$ yards backing
51" x 51" batting

CUTTING

Nine-Patch-in-a-Square Block (49)

From the assorted small prints, cut three $1^7/8$" x 42" strips each. Cut each strip in half crosswise, for 54 total (A).

From the light and the dark prints, cut five 4" x 42" strips each. Cut into 49 light and 49 dark 4" squares; cut diagonally in half for 98 light and 98 dark triangles (B).

Border

From the red bandana stripe print, cut *on the lengthwise grain* four $2^1/2$" x $51^1/2$" strips.

ASSEMBLY

1. Select nine different A strips. Sew them together in sets of three. Press two sets toward the outer edges (for rows 1 and 3) and one set toward the middle (for row 2). Cut each set into ten $1^7/8$" segments.

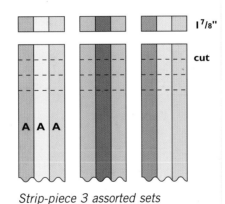

Strip-piece 3 assorted sets

2. Lay out the segments for rows 1, 2, and 3. Sew the rows together, butting the seams. Press. Make ten units total, rotating rows 1 and 3 on some of them for greater variety.

Row 1

Row 2

Row 3

Join the segments

3. Repeat steps 1 and 2, sewing different combinations each time, until you have used up all the strips and have 49 Nine-Patch units total.

4. Stitch two light B triangles to opposite edges of each Nine-Patch. Press. Stitch two dark B triangles to the remaining edges. Press. Trim to $6^1/2$" square (for a 6" finished size).

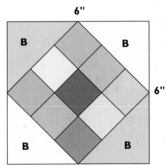

Nine-Patch-in-a-Square
Make 49 assorted

5. Lay out the blocks in seven rows of seven blocks each, as shown in the quilt diagram (page 112). Position the lighter triangles at the top right and lower left corners of each block, as shown in the quilt photograph. Stitch the blocks together in rows. Press. Join the rows together. Press.

6. Pin the side borders to the quilt, letting the excess extend evenly at each end. Sew together, starting and stopping $1/4$" from the top and bottom edges of the quilt. Repeat to join the top and bottom borders. Miter the corners, and trim off the excess border fabric.

7. Layer and finish the quilt. In *Nostalgic Nine-Patch*, the patches are outline-quilted and an X design is stitched in the middle square of each block.

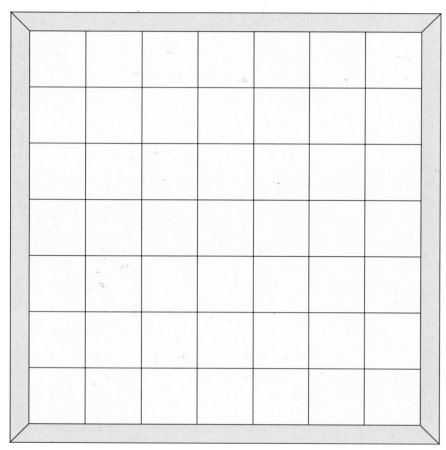

Quilt Diagram

Favorite Quilt

Designed by Jean Wells. Block size, 12"; quilt size, 60¹/₂" x 72¹/₂".

Aunt Vina's Favorite blocks are joined without sashing to create this lively quilt design. The secondary pattern is so strong, it's hard to tell where the original block design begins and ends. I have been collecting black and cream little prints for years, and this quilt gave me a chance to use them, creating the look of an antique quilt.

BASIC INSTRUCTIONS

Aunt Vina's Favorite (page 106)
Straight Set (page 43)
Finishing a Quilt (page 46)

MATERIALS

Assorted small prints:

$2^3/4$ yards total black-on-cream

$2^3/8$ yards total cream-on-black

$^3/4$ yard total gold

$^1/2$ yard black solid for binding

$3^2/3$ yards backing

65" x 77" batting

CUTTING

From the cream-on-black small prints, cut four $4^1/2$" x 42" strips. Cut into thirty $4^1/2$" squares (A).

From the cream-on-black and black-on-cream small prints, cut eight $4^7/8$" x 42" strips each, or 16 total. Cut each strip in half crosswise. Layer the strips right sides together in black/cream pairs, making as many different combinations as possible. Cut into 60 layered $4^7/8$" squares; cut diagonally in half for 120 layered triangles (B, C). Do not separate the pairs; they are ready for sewing.

From the gold and the cream-on-black small prints, cut eleven $1^7/8$" x 42" strips each. Cut each strip in half crosswise (D, E).

From the black-on-cream small prints, cut eighteen $2^7/8$" x 42" strips. Cut into two hundred forty $2^7/8$" squares; cut diagonally in half (F).

ASSEMBLY

1. Stitch the B and C triangles together as paired. Press. Trim the ears.

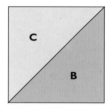

Make 120 assorted

2. Stitch the D and E strips together in pairs, making as many combinations as possible. Press. Cut each set into ten $1^7/8$" segments. Stitch the segments together in random pairs to make 120 Four-Patch units. Press. Stitch 4 F triangles to each unit. Press.

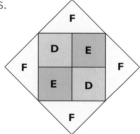

Make 120 assorted

3. Join the A, BC, and DEF units to make 30 Aunt Vina's Favorite blocks. Be sure to position the gold D squares as shown in the quilt photograph (page 113) and block diagram. To ensure a scrappy look and to avoid repetition, lay out and complete four

identical blocks at a time. For each new batch of four, choose a different fabric arrangement.

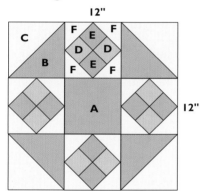

Aunt Vina's Favorite Block
Make 30 assorted

4. Lay out the blocks in six rows of five blocks each, as shown in the quilt diagram. Stitch the blocks together in rows. Press. Join the rows. Press.

5. Layer and finish the quilt. In *Favorite Quilt*, the Four-Patches in each block are outline-quilted, a petal motif is quilted in the center square, and teardrops fill the light-colored squares formed by the block corners. The quilting enhances the circular flow of the patchwork within each block.

Quilt Diagram

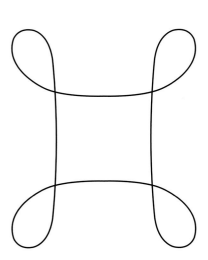

Favorite Quilt Petal Quilting Design

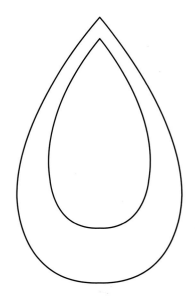

Favorite Quilt Teardrops Quilting Design

CHAPTER 6

Small Triangles

*A*s the patchwork pieces get smaller, the block complexity increases. Chaining can help you achieve both speed and accuracy when you need to turn out half-square triangles by the dozens.

BEAR'S PAW

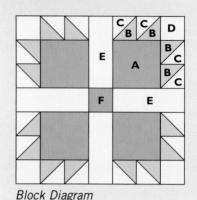

Block Diagram

The Bear's Paw block is made up of four square "paw" units that are joined by sashing strips and a small square at the center. Half-square triangles around the edges of the block form the claws on each paw. There are lots of these small triangles, but chaining makes the sewing go faster. You'll find yourself developing a rhythm and becoming more efficient with each batch you make.

FOR A 12" BLOCK, CUT:

four $3^3/4$" squares (A)

eight $2^1/2$" squares, cut diagonally in half (B)

eight $2^1/2$" squares, cut diagonally in half (C)

four $2^1/8$" squares (D)

four $2^3/4$" x $5^3/8$" rectangles (E)

one $2^3/4$" square (F)

FOR A 10^1/2" BLOCK, CUT:

four $3^1/2$" squares (A)

eight $2^3/8$" squares, cut diagonally in half (B)

eight $2^3/8$" squares, cut diagonally in half (C)

four 2" squares (D)

four 2" x 5" rectangles (E)

one 2" square (F)

FOR AN 8^1/2" BLOCK, CUT:

four 3" squares (A)

eight $2^1/8$" squares, cut diagonally in half (B)

eight $2^1/8$" squares, cut diagonally in half (C)

four $1^3/4$" squares (D)

four $1^1/2$" x $4^1/4$" rectangles (E)

one $1^1/2$" square (F)

---

1. Chain-stitch the B and C triangles together in pairs. Clip apart. Press toward the darker fabric. Trim off the ears.

Make 16

2. Stitch the BC units together in pairs, making half of them in mirror image. Press. Add D squares to four units as shown.

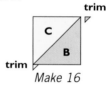

Make 4

Make 4

3. Lay out one A square, one BC claw strip, and one BCD claw strip as shown. Stitch the shorter claw strip to the right edge of A. Press toward A. Stitch the longer claw strip to the top edge. Press. Make four units total.

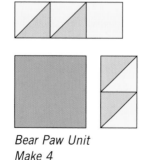

Bear Paw Unit
Make 4

4. Lay out the four paw units in a square so that the claws face out toward the corners. Insert sashing strips E and center square F in between as shown. Stitch the pieces together in rows. Press toward E. Join the rows together, butting the seams. Press.

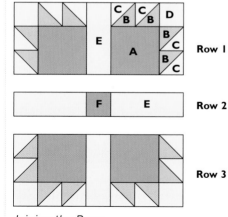

Row 1

Row 2

Row 3

Joining the Rows

FRUIT BASKET

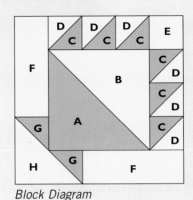

Block Diagram

The Fruit Basket block can be set on point or on its side, as shown here. Since this block is based on a 5x5 grid, the cutting sizes for a 12" block are a bit off. Using a scant $1/4$" seam allowance when you sew the 12" block will help offset the discrepancy.

FOR A 12" BLOCK, CUT:

one 8" square, cut diagonally in half (A)
  (use one triangle)
one 8" square, cut diagonally in half (B)
  (use one triangle)
three $3^1/4$" squares, cut diagonally in half (C)
three $3^1/4$" squares, cut diagonally in half (D)
one $2^7/8$" square (E)
two $2^7/8$" x $7^5/8$" rectangles (F)
one $3^1/4$" square, cut diagonally in half (G)
one $5^5/8$" square, cut diagonally in half (H)
  (use one triangle)

FOR A 10" BLOCK, CUT:

one $6^7/8$" square, cut diagonally in half (A)
  (use one triangle)
one $6^7/8$" square, cut diagonally in half (B)
  (use one triangle)
three $2^7/8$" squares, cut diagonally in half (C)
three $2^7/8$" squares, cut diagonally in half (D)
one $2^1/2$" square (E)
two $2^1/2$" x $6^1/2$" rectangles (F)
one $2^7/8$" square, cut diagonally in half (G)
one $4^7/8$" triangle, cut diagonally in half (H)
  (use one triangle)

FOR A $7^1/2$" BLOCK, CUT:

one $5^3/8$" square, cut diagonally in half (A)
  (use one triangle)
one $5^3/8$" square, cut diagonally in half (B)
  (use one triangle)
three $2^3/8$" squares, cut diagonally in half (C)
three $2^3/8$" squares, cut diagonally in half (D)
one 2" square (E)
two 2" x 5" rectangles (F)
one $2^3/8$" square, cut diagonally in half (G)
one $3^7/8$" triangle, cut diagonally in half (H)
  (use one triangle)

1. Stitch the A and B triangles together. Press toward the darker fabric. Trim off the ears.

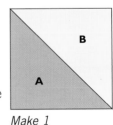

Make 1

2. Chain-stitch the C and D triangles together in pairs. Clip apart and press. Trim off the ears. Stitch the CD units together in two groups of three, making one set in mirror image. Add an E square to one set as shown. Press.

Make 1

Make 1

3. Stitch a G to each F, making two mirror-image units. Press.

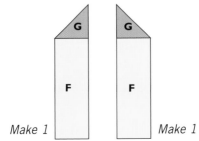

Make 1   *Make 1*

4. Lay out all of the pieced units and triangle H. Stitch the seams in the order shown, pressing after each addition.

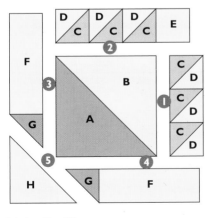

Joining the Pieces

The Oregon Trail

Designed by Jean Wells. Block size, 12"; quilt size, 64" x 77¹/₂".

The Bear's Paw block is an all-time favorite. In this variation, the center square fabric matches the paws and an accent color is used for the claws. All of the fabrics are batiks, lending a contemporary mood to a quilter's classic.

BASIC INSTRUCTIONS

Bear's Paw Block (page 118)
Straight Set (page 43)
Finishing a Quilt (page 46)

MATERIALS

$2^1/_4$ yards burgundy batik
2 yards pale yellow batik
$7/_8$ yard deep sage green batik
$1^1/_8$ yards rust batik
$1/_2$ yard for binding
$3^7/_8$ yards backing
68" x 82" batting

CUTTING

Bear's Paw Blocks (20)

From the burgundy batik, cut eight $3^3/_4$" x 42" strips. Cut into eighty $3^3/_4$" squares (A). Cut two $2^3/_8$" x 42" strips. Cut into twenty $2^3/_4$" squares (F).

From the pale yellow batik, cut five $2^1/_8$" x 42" strips. Cut into eighty $2^1/_8$" squares (D). Cut twelve $2^3/_4$" x 42" strips. Cut into eighty $2^3/_4$" x $5^3/_8$" rectangles (E).

From the deep sage green batik and the pale yellow batik, cut ten $2^1/_2$" x 42" strips each. Place the strips right sides together in green/yellow pairs. Cut into 160 layered $2^1/_2$" squares. Cut diagonally in half for 320 layered triangles (B, C). Do not separate the pairs; they are ready for sewing.

Sashing and Inner Border

From the rust batik, cut seventeen 2" x 42" strips. Cut into fifteen 2" x $12^1/_2$" strips for the vertical sashing. Sew the remaining pieces into one long strip. Cut into six 2" x 53" strips for the horizontal sashing and the top and bottom inner borders two 2" x $69^1/_2$" strips for the side inner borders.

Outer Border

From the burgundy batik, cut seven $4^1/_2$" x 42" strips. Sew into one long strip. Cut into two $4^1/_2$" x $69^1/_2$" strips for the side outer borders and two $4^1/_2$" x 64" strips for the top and bottom outer borders.

ASSEMBLY

1. Sew pieces A through F together to make 20 Bear's Paw blocks.

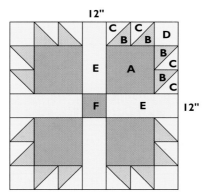

Bear's Paw Block
Make 20

2. Lay out the blocks in five rows of four blocks each. Stitch the blocks together in rows, inserting vertical sashing strips in between. Press toward the sashing. Join the rows together, inserting horizontal sashing strips in between. Press.

3. Sew the top and bottom inner borders to the quilt top. Press. Add the side inner borders. Press. Add the side outer borders. Press. Add the top and bottom outer borders. Press.

4. Layer and finish the quilt. In *The Oregon Trail*, each Bear's Paw is outline-quilted and simple swirls decorate the blocks and border.

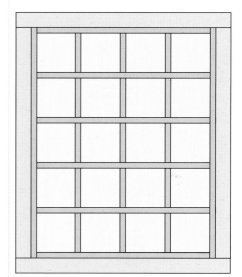

Quilt Diagram

Twilight Bear's Paw

Designed by Jean Wells. Block size, 8$\frac{1}{2}$"; quilt size, 28" x 40".

Solid black Bear's Paws recede into the background in this dramatic setting. The rich jewel-toned and pastel palette, set against a black ground, was inspired by antique Amish quilts. In this interpretation, red fabric accentuates the binding.

BASIC INSTRUCTIONS

Bear's Paw Block (page 118)
Diagonal Set (page 44)
Finishing a Quilt (page 46)

MATERIALS

$1^1/2$ yards black
$^1/4$ yard each red, magenta, aqua, green, and lavender
$^1/4$ yard red for binding
$1^1/4$ yards backing
32" x 44" batting

CUTTING

Bear's Paw Blocks (8)

From the black, cut three 3" x 42" strips. Cut into thirty-two 3" squares (A). Cut four $2^1/8$" x 42" strips. Cut each strip in half for eight total (B). Cut one $1^1/2$" x 13" strip. Cut into eight $1^1/2$" squares (F).

Cut the red, magenta, aqua, green, and lavender quarter-yard cuts in half, for two 9" x 21" pieces each. Set aside one green and one lavender piece for another project. From each of the eight remaining pieces, cut one $2^1/8$" x 21" strip (C). Cut one $1^3/4$" x 21" strip. Cut into four $1^3/4$" squares (D). Cut one $1^1/2$" x 21" strip. Cut into four $1^1/2$" x $4^1/4$" strips (E).

Layer the B and C strips right sides together in black/colored pairs. Cut into eight layered $2^1/8$" squares per set, or 64 total. Cut diagonally in half for 128 layered triangles (B, C).

Do not separate the pairs; they are ready for sewing.

Setting Triangles

From the black, cut one $13^1/4$" x 42" strip. Cut into two $13^1/4$" squares; cut diagonally in both directions for six setting triangles (two are discarded). From the leftover strip, cut two $6^7/8$" squares; cut diagonally in half for four corner setting triangles.

Border

From the black, cut four $2^1/4$" x 42" strips. Cut into two $2^1/4$" x $24^1/2$" strips for the top and bottom borders and two $2^1/4$" x 40" strips for the side borders.

ASSEMBLY

1. Sew pieces A through F together to make eight Bear's Paw blocks: two red, two magenta, two aqua, one green, and one lavender.

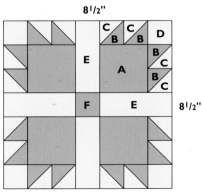

Bear's Paw Block
Make 8 assorted

2. Lay out the blocks on point, as shown in the the quilt photograph and quilt diagram (page 124). Place the setting triangles around the edges. Stitch the blocks and setting triangles together in diagonal rows. Press. Sew the rows together. Press. Add the corner triangles. Press.

3. Sew the top and bottom borders to the quilt top. Press. Add the side borders. Press.

4. Layer and finish the quilt. In *Twilight Bear's Paw*, outline quilting defines the patchwork shapes. Use the pattern on page 124 to quilt the setting triangles and border. Red binding adds a contrasting note around the edges.

Quilt Diagram

Make a mirror image copy to complete the pattern

binding edge

Twilight Bear's Paw Quilting Design

Betsy's Baskets

Designed by Jean Wells and Betsy Mennesson. Block size, 10"; quilt size, 83$\frac{1}{2}$" x 83$\frac{1}{2}$".

Pictures of Provence, France, provided the pattern and color ideas for the fabrics in this quilt. The palette is predominantly blues and yellows, with reds and greens popping up in smaller amounts. The plaid inner border was cut on the bias to increase the visual texture.

BASIC INSTRUCTIONS

Fruit Basket Block (page 119)
Diagonal Set (page 44)
Finishing a Quilt (page 46)

MATERIALS

Basket blocks:

2 yards total assorted white-background prints

$1/4$ yard blue plaid

$1/4$ yard olive green plaid

$1/4$ yard each two different dark blue prints

$1/8$ yard each four different textured solids in yellow, red, and blue

Setting triangles:

$1^5/8$ yards total assorted yellow small prints

1 yard total assorted blue small prints

$1^5/8$ yards dark blue print (can match basket fabric)

$5/8$ yard olive green plaid (can match basket fabric)

$1/2$ yard for binding

$7^1/2$ yards backing

88" x 88" batting

CUTTING

Fruit Basket Blocks (25)

Follow the directions to cut pieces A through H for four blocks. Repeat the cutting sequence six times, using a different combination of fabrics each time. Then cut for one more block, using the 10" cutting guide on page 119, to bring the block total to 25.

From a plaid or a print, cut two $6^7/8$" squares; cut diagonally in half (A). Cut four $2^7/8$" squares; cut diagonally in half (G).

From the white-background fabric, cut two $6^7/8$" squares; cut diagonally in half (B). Cut two $2^1/2$" x 42" strips. Cut into four $2^1/2$" squares (E) and eight $2^1/2$" x $6^1/2$" rectangles (F). Cut two $4^7/8$" squares; cut diagonally in half (H).

From a textured solid and the same white-background print, cut one $2^7/8$" x 42" strip each. Layer the strips right sides together. Cut into 12 layered $2^7/8$" squares; cut diagonally in half for 24 layered triangles (C, D). Do not separate the pairs; they are ready for sewing.

Setting Triangles

From the assorted small prints, cut six yellow and four blue $15^3/8$" squares; cut diagonally in both directions for 24 yellow and 16 blue setting triangles. Cut six yellow and four blue 8" squares; cut diagonally in half for 12 yellow and 8 blue corner triangles.

Borders

From the olive green plaid, cut a 21" square. Cut diagonally in half. Following the directions on page 128, sew the triangles together and cut a $1^1/4$"-wide continuous bias strip. Cut into two $1^1/4$" x $71^1/8$" strips for the side inner borders and two $1^1/4$" x $72^5/8$" strips for the top and bottom inner borders. Avoid stretching the bias edge as you measure and cut.

From the dark blue print, cut nine 6" x 42" strips. Sew together into one long strip. Cut into two 6" x $72^5/8$" strips for the side outer borders and two 6" x $83^5/8$" strips for the top and bottom outer borders.

ASSEMBLY

1. Sew pieces A through H together to make 25 Fruit Basket blocks. As you work, swap some of the C pieces between blocks to create multicolored handles.

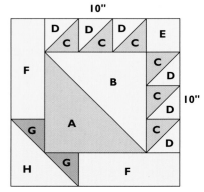

Fruit Basket Block
Make 25 assorted

2. Lay out the blocks on point in five columns of five blocks each. Place the setting triangles in between, using yellow in columns 1, 3, and 5 and blue in columns 2 and 4, as shown in the quilt photograph (page 125) and quilt diagram. Add the corner triangles to the top and bottom of each column, matching the colors. Adjust the arrangement as needed so that similar fabrics are not clustered together.

3. Stitch the yellow and blue setting triangles and corner triangles together along their shared seam lines. Press toward the darker fabric.

4. Stitch the blocks and triangles together in diagonal rows. Press toward the triangles. Join the rows together. Press. Add the four remaining corner triangles. Press.

5. Sew the side inner borders to the quilt top, pinning first and being careful not to stretch the bias edge. Press. Sew the top and bottom inner borders. Press. Add the side outer borders. Press. Add the top and bottom outer borders. Press.

6. Layer and finish the quilt. In *Betsy's Baskets*, outline quilting defines the baskets and free-motion quilting designs fill them. The setting triangles also feature free-motion patterns.

Column I	Column 2	Column 3	Column 4	Column 5

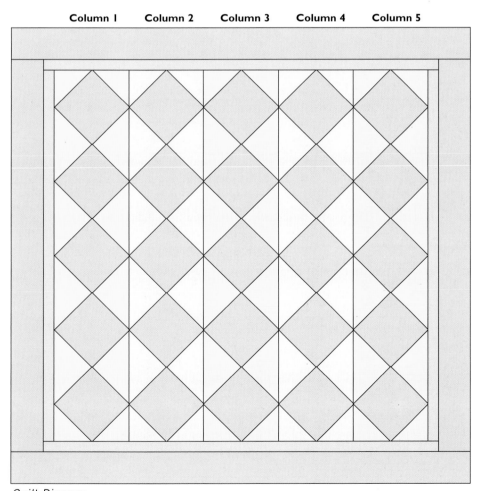

Quilt Diagram

✛ CUTTING A BIAS STRIP

Plaids and stripes are especially effective when cut on the bias. Use this method when your project calls for long bias-cut strips.

1. Cut a square of fabric 18" or larger. Cut diagonally in half, making two triangles. Place the triangles right sides together, matching two straight-grain edges as shown. Stitch together with a $^1/_4$" seam allowance. Press the seam allowance open.

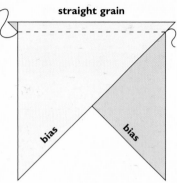

Join the half-square triangles

2. Lay the piece wrong side up on a flat, hard surface. Align your cutting ruler on one bias-cut edge and measure the desired strip width, just as you would for rotary cutting. Instead of cutting, run a pencil or fabric marker along the edge of the ruler. Continue measuring and marking parallel lines one strip width apart. Starting at point A, cut on the first marked line for about 5".

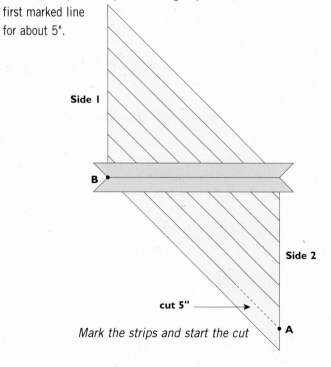

Mark the strips and start the cut

3. Bring side 1 and side 2 right sides together, matching point A to point B. Pin so that the marked lines offset one another by one strip width and the cut end dangles free. The piece will be awkward to handle at this stage. Stitch $^1/_4$" from the edge and press the seam allowance open, creating a tube.

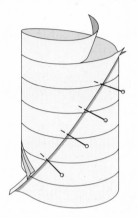

Sew a tube, offsetting the strips

4. Continue the cut begun in step 2, following the marked lines through the seams, to make one continuous bias strip.

Kitschy Baskets

Designed by Jean Wells. Block size, 12"; quilt size, 42½" x 42½".

The retro fruit print for these baskets came from a pair of reproduction cloth napkins. Popular in the 1940s, fruit and flower motifs like these are making a comeback in home decorating. If you don't want to use napkins, a retro-style fruit print fabric can be substituted.

BASIC INSTRUCTIONS

Fruit Basket Block (page 119)
Diagonal Set (page 44)
Finishing a Quilt (page 46)

MATERIALS

two 16"-square printed cotton napkins
(design must appear in all four
corners as shown at right)
$7/8$ yard red floral print
$3/4$ yard blue textured solid
$5/8$ yard small fruit print on white
$1/4$ yard medium fruit print on white
$1/4$ yard yellow textured solid
$3/8$ yard for binding
$1^3/4$ yards backing
47" x 47" batting

CUTTING

Fruit Basket Blocks (5)

Cut each napkin into four 8" squares.
Cut each square diagonally in half.
Select five napkin corners for the
baskets (A). From the leftover napkin
fabric, cut five $3^1/4$" squares; cut
diagonally in half (G).

From the red floral print, cut one 8" x
42" strip. Cut into three 8" squares.
Cut each square diagonally in
half (B).

From the medium fruit print on white
and the blue textured solid, cut two
$3^1/4$" x 42" strips each. Place the
strips right sides together in white/
blue pairs. Cut into 15 layered $3^1/4$"
squares; cut diagonally in half for
30 layered triangles (C, D). Do not
separate the pairs; they are ready
for sewing.

From the blue textured solid, cut one
$2^7/8$" x 21" strip. Cut into five $2^7/8$"
squares (E). Cut two $2^7/8$" x 42"
strips. Cut into ten $2^7/8$" x $7^5/8$"
rectangles (F). Cut one $5^5/8$" x 21"
strip. Cut into three $5^5/8$" squares;
cut diagonally in half (H).

Setting Triangles

From the small fruit print on white, cut
one $18^1/4$" square; cut diagonally in
both directions for four setting triangles. Cut two $9^3/8$" squares; cut
diagonally in half for four corner
setting triangles.

Borders

From the yellow textured solid, cut
four $1^1/2$" x 42" strips. Cut into two
$1^1/2$" x $34^1/2$" strips for the side
inner borders and two $1^1/2$" x $36^1/2$"
strips for the top and bottom inner
borders.

From the red floral print, cut five
$3^1/2$" x 42" strips. Sew into one long
strip. Cut into two $3^1/2$" x $36^1/2$"
strips for the side outer borders
and two $3^1/2$" x $42^1/2$" strips for the
top and bottom outer borders.

ASSEMBLY

1. Sew pieces A through H together to make five Fruit Basket blocks.

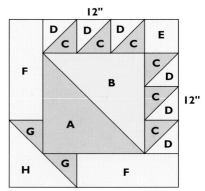

Fruit Basket Block
Make 5 assorted

2. Lay out the blocks on point, forming an X pattern, as shown in the quilt photograph (page 129) and quilt diagram. Place the setting triangles and corner triangles around the edges. Stitch the blocks and setting triangles together in diagonal rows. Press. Sew the rows together. Press. Add the corner triangles. Press.

3. Sew the side inner borders to the quilt top. Press. Add the top and bottom inner borders. Press. Add the side outer borders. Press. Add the top and bottom outer borders. Press.

4. Layer and finish the quilt. Each basket in *Kitschy Baskets* is quilted ¼" from the edge, creating an outline. The red print fabric inspired the daisy quilting design in the setting triangles.

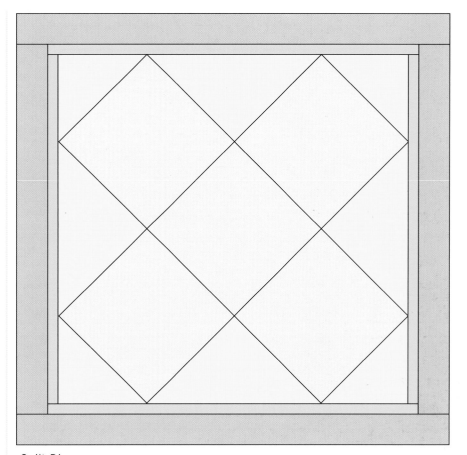

Quilt Diagram

Kitschy Baskets Daisy Quilting Design

Picture Blocks

*T*he multiple pieces in a picture block fit together like a puzzle. Make houses and trees using squares, rectangles, triangles, and shapes cut from templates. Picture blocks are especially fun for trying out new color and fabric combinations.

HOUSE

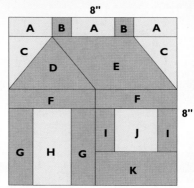

8"

| A | B | A | B | A |

| C | | | | C |
| | D | | E | |

| F | | F | |

| I | J | I |

| G | H | G |

| K |

8"

Block Diagram

T he House block contains 18 patchwork pieces. To avoid confusion, lay out all the pieces and sew them together row by row. Row 3 is assembled in two sections to create the door and window.

FOR AN 8" BLOCK:

Prepare templates C, D, and E (pages 138–139).

Cut the following pieces:

three $2^1/2$" x $1^1/2$" rectangles (A)

two $1^1/2$" squares (B)

2 C (reverse one)

1 D

1 E

two $4^1/2$" x $1^1/2$" rectangles (F)

two $1^3/4$" x 4" rectangles (G)

one 2" x 4" rectangle (H)

two $1^1/2$" x $2^1/2$" rectangles (I)

one $2^1/2$" square (J)

one $4^1/2$" x 2" rectangle (K)

1. Lay out pieces A through K in order next to your sewing machine, referring to the block diagram.

2. Stitch B to A. Press toward B. Repeat. Join 2 AB units and 1 A. Press.

3. Stitch D to E. Press toward the darker fabric. Stitch a C to each outer edge. Press.

4. Stitch 2 G's to opposite sides of H. Press. Add F to the top edge of GHG. Press. Stitch 2 I's to opposite edges of J. Press. Add F to the top edge. Press. Add K to the bottom edge. Press. Join the two units together. Press.

5. Join rows 1, 2, and 3, pressing after each addition.

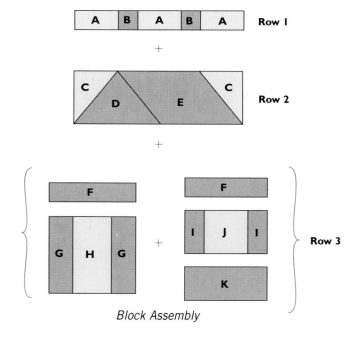

Block Assembly

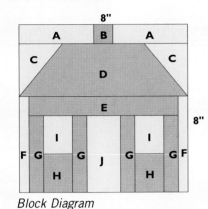

BASIC BLOCK # COTTAGE

Block Diagram

T he Cottage block features a door and two windows—perfect places for using special fabrics. Narrow strips of background fabric at both ends of row 3 help define the roof overhang.

FOR AN 8" BLOCK:

Prepare templates C and D (page 138).

Cut the following pieces:

two 4" x $1^1/2$" rectangles (A)

one $1^1/2$" square (B)

2 C (reverse one)

1 D

one $7^1/2$" x $1^1/2$" rectangle (E)

two 1" x 5" rectangles (F)

four $1^1/4$" x 4" rectangles (G)

two $1^3/4$" x $2^1/4$" rectangles (H)

two $1^3/4$" x $2^1/4$" rectangles (I)

one 2" x 4" rectangle (J)

1. Lay out pieces A through J in order next to your sewing machine, referring to the block diagram.

2. Stitch the A's to opposite edges of B. Press toward B.

3. Stitch the C's to D. Press toward D.

4. Stitch H and I together in pairs along the shorter edges. Press. Add 2 G's to each HI. Press. Join the units together, inserting J in between. Press. Add E to the top edge. Press. Add the F's to the side edges. Press.

5. Join rows 1, 2, and 3, pressing after each addition.

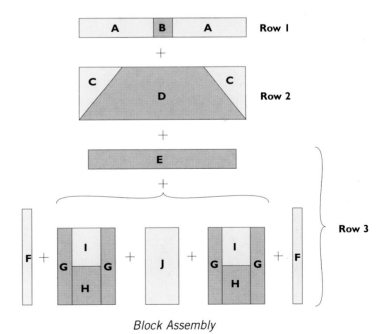

Block Assembly

PINE TREE

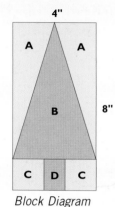

Block Diagram

The rectangular Pine Tree block is assembled in two rows.

FOR A 4" X 8" BLOCK:

Prepare templates A and B (pages 138–139).

Cut the following pieces:

 2 A (reverse one)

 1 B

 two 2" squares (C)

 one $1^{1}/_{2}$" x 2" rectangle (D)

1. Lay out pieces A through D in order next to your sewing machine, referring to the block diagram.

2. Place A on B, right sides together and dots matching. Pin. Stitch from the bottom of the tree to the top. Flip A over the seam allowance and press lightly from the right side, taking care not to stretch the fabric.

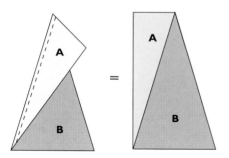

3. Repeat step 2 to sew the mirror image A to the other side of B.

4. Stitch 2 C's to opposite edges of D. Press toward D.

5. Join rows 1 and 2. Press toward the tree.

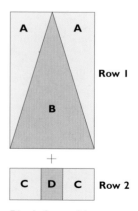

Block Assembly

APPLE TREE

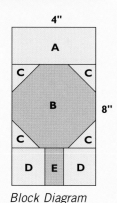

4"

A

C   C

B   8"

C   C

D E D

Block Diagram

The rectangular Apple Tree block is assembled in three rows. Row 1 represents the sky, giving this tree a short appearance. Use the Flying Geese method (page 87) to add the corner triangles that shape the tree. No templates are needed.

FOR A 4" X 8" BLOCK, CUT:

one $4^1/_2$" x $2^1/_2$" rectangle (A)

one $4^1/_2$" square (B)

four $1^1/_2$" squares (C)

two 2" x $2^1/_2$" rectangles (D)

one $1^1/_2$" x $2^1/_2$" rectangle (E)

1. Fold each C square diagonally in half, right side out, and press to set the crease. Unfold. Place C on a corner of B, right sides together. Stitch on the diagonal fold line through both layers. Trim $^1/_4$" beyond the stitching. Flip C over the seam allowance and press from the right side. Repeat for each corner.

2. Stitch 2 D's to opposite edges of E. Press toward E.

3. Join rows 1, 2, and 3, pressing after each addition.

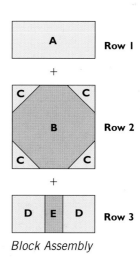

Block Assembly

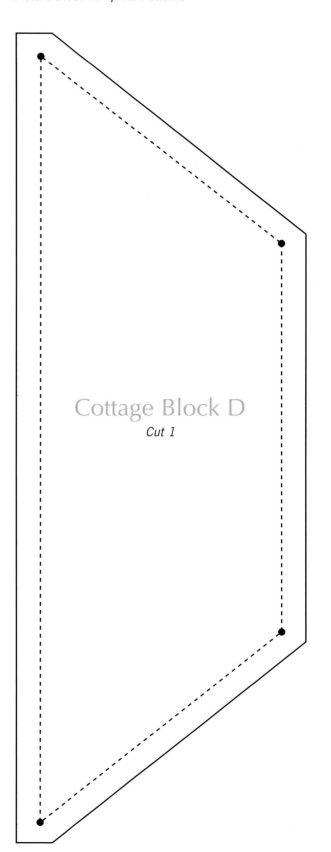

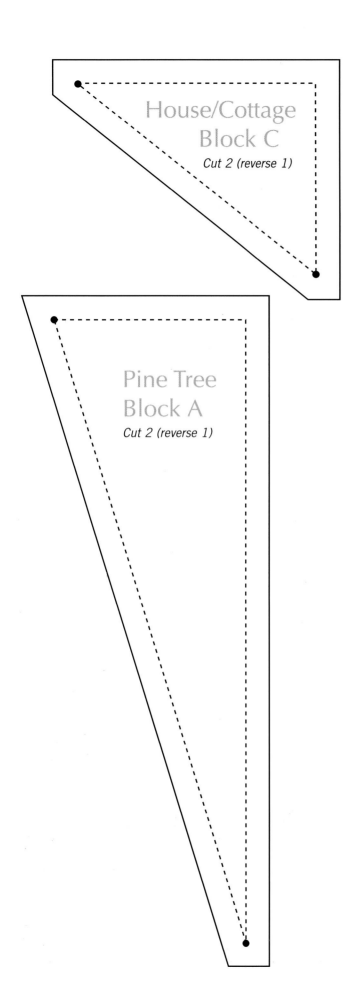

House/Cottage
Block C
Cut 2 (reverse 1)

Picture Block Template Patterns

Pine Tree
Block A
Cut 2 (reverse 1)

Cottage Block D
Cut 1

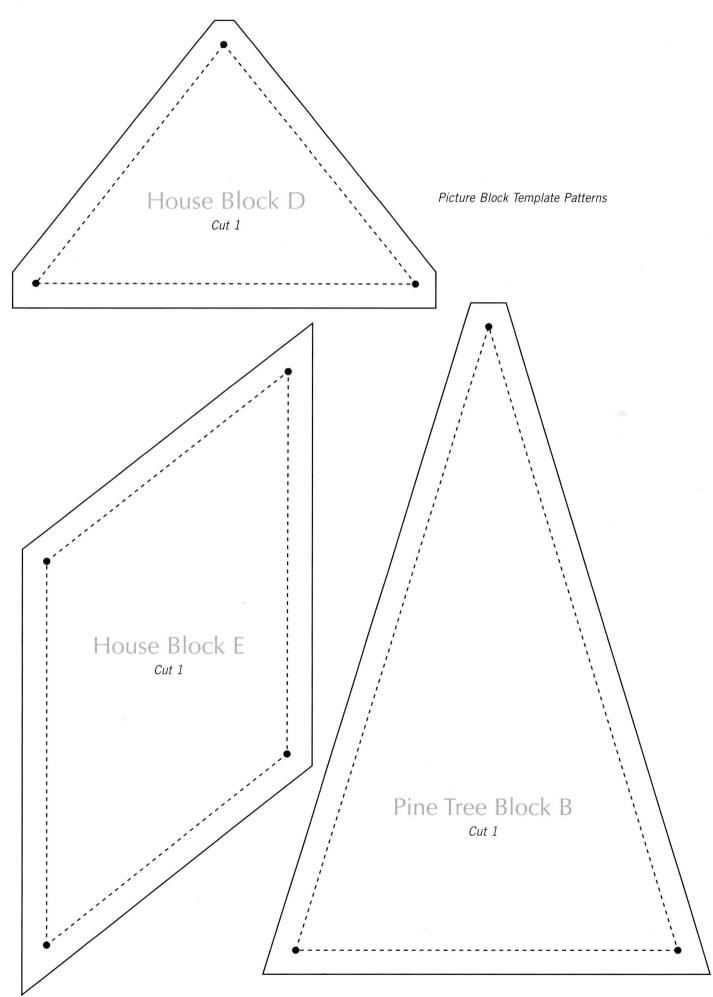

House Block D
Cut 1

Picture Block Template Patterns

House Block E
Cut 1

Pine Tree Block B
Cut 1

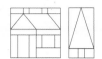

Pinebrook

Designed by Jean Wells. House block size, 8"; Pine Tree block size, 4" x 8"; quilt size, 36$\frac{1}{2}$" x 36$\frac{1}{2}$".

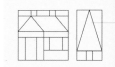

Create a town-and-country landscape with this medallion-style setting. In the middle of the quilt, four "village" houses are fenced in with a blue border and sashing. Four "country" houses and a forest of pine trees surround them. Plaids and small prints were chosen for the images.

BASIC INSTRUCTIONS

House Block (page 134)
Pine Tree Block (page 136)
Straight Set (page 43)
Finishing a Quilt (page 46)

MATERIALS

2 yards total assorted red, blue, and green small plaids and prints
$1^1/8$ yards off-white solid
$1/4$ yard red solid
$1/4$ yard blue solid
$1/8$ yard small gray plaid
$1/4$ yard for binding
$1^1/8$ yards backing
41" x 41" batting

CUTTING

House Blocks (8)

Prepare House templates C, D, and E (pages 138–139).

From the off-white, cut two $1^1/2$" x 42" strips. Cut into eight $1^1/2$" x $5^1/2$" rectangles (A1) and eight $1^1/2$" x $2^1/2$" rectangles (A2). Cut one 3" x 42" strip, fold in half, ride side in, and cut 8 C through both layers, or 16 total (eight in reverse).

From the red solid, cut one $1^1/2$" x 42" strip. Cut into eight $1^1/2$" squares (B). Cut one 2" x 42" strip. Cut into eight 2" x 4" rectangles (H). Cut one $2^1/2$" x 42" strip. Cut into eight $2^1/2$" squares (J).

From the assorted plaids and prints, cut 8 D, 8 E, sixteen $1^1/2$" x $4^1/2$" rectangles (F), sixteen $1^3/4$" x 4" rectangles (G), sixteen $1^1/2$" x $2^1/2$"

rectangles (I), and eight 2" x $4^1/2$" rectangles (K). Refer to the quilt photograph for color ideas. In this quilt, each house block uses one fabric for pieces D, F, and G and a coordinating fabric for pieces F, I, and K. The chimneys, windows, and doors are solid red.

Pine Tree Blocks (20)

From the off-white, cut three $7^1/2$" x 42" strips. Fold the strips in half, right side in, and cut 20 A through both layers, or 40 total (20 in reverse). Cut two 2" x 42" strips. Cut into forty 2" squares (C).

From the assorted plaids and prints, cut 20 B. Stack the fabrics to speed the cutting.

From the small gray plaid, cut one 2" x 42" strip. Cut into twenty 2" x $1^1/2$" rectangles (D).

Sashing and Inner Border

From the blue solid, cut one 2" x 42" strip. Cut into two 2" x $8^1/2$" strips for the vertical sashing and one 2" x 18" strip for the horizontal sashing. Cut two $1^3/4$" x 42" strips. Cut into two $1^3/4$" x 18" strips for the top and bottom inner borders and two $1^3/4$" x $20^1/2$" strips for the side inner borders.

ASSEMBLY

1. Join house pieces A through K to make eight blocks. In this version of the block, there is only one chimney, placed off-center.

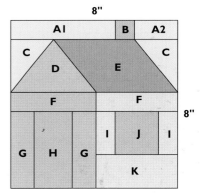

*House Block
Make 8*

2. Join pine tree pieces A through D to make 20 blocks.

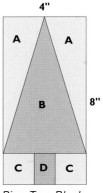

*Pine Tree Block
Make 20*

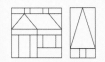

3. Lay out four house blocks, juxta-posing the red and blue roofs as shown in the quilt photograph (page 140). Stitch together in rows, insert-ing vertical sashing strips in between. Press. Join the rows, horizontal sash-ing strip, and top and bottom inner borders. Press. Add the side inner borders. Press.

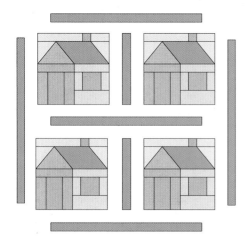

4. Stitch five Pine Tree blocks side by side; repeat to make four borders total. Stitch two tree borders to the sides of the quilt top, trees pointing inward. Press. Stitch two House blocks to each remaining tree border, turning one set of trees upside down, as shown in the quilt photograph (page 140). Press. Sew the house/tree borders to the top and bottom edges of the quilt, trees pointing inward. Press.

5. Layer and finish the quilt. *Pinebrook* was stitched in-the-ditch between the blocks.

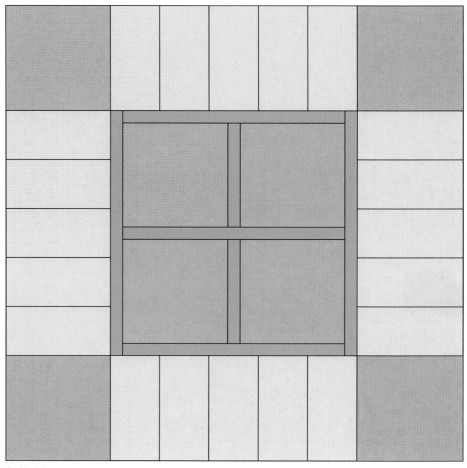

Quilt Diagram

■ **House block**

□ **Pine Tree block**

 # Emily's Cottage

Designed by Jean Wells. Cottage block size, 8"; Apple Tree block size, 4" x 8"; quilt size, 28$\frac{1}{2}$" x 36$\frac{1}{2}$".

Emily's Cottage is a floral fantasy. All of the fabrics in the trees and cottage have a floral feel—even the rose-colored chimney! Some show subtle floral textures, others are more high-contrast. The result is an unexpectedly delightful melange.

BASIC INSTRUCTIONS

Cottage Block (page 135)
Apple Tree Block (page 137)
Straight Set (page 43)
Finishing a Quilt (page 46)

MATERIALS

2/3 yard pink/olive floral print
3/8 yard small rose-on-cream print
1/4 yard medium rose print
1/4 yard tan small print
1/4 yard yellow textured solid
1/4 yard dark mauve large print
1/4 yard sage green large print
1/4 yard for binding
1 yard backing
33" x 42" batting

CUTTING

Cottage Blocks (4)

Prepare Cottage templates C and D (page 138).

From the small rose-on-cream print, cut one 1¹/₂" x 42" strip. Cut into eight 1¹/₂" x 4¹/₂" rectangles (A). Cut one 3" x 42" strip. Fold in half, right side in, and cut 4 C through both layers, or 8 total (four in reverse). Cut one 1" x 42" strip. Cut into eight 1" x 5" rectangles (F).

From the medium rose print, cut four 1¹/₂" squares (B).

From the tan small print, cut 4 D.

From the pink/olive floral print, cut four 1¹/₂" x 7¹/₂" rectangles (E), sixteen 1¹/₄" x 4" rectangles (G), and eight 1³/₄" x 2¹/₄" rectangles (H).

From the yellow textured solid, cut eight 1³/₄ x 2¹/₄" rectangles (I).

From the dark mauve large print, cut four 2" x 4" rectangles (J).

Apple Tree Blocks (4)

From the small rose-on-cream print, cut one 2¹/₂" x 42" strip. Cut into four 2¹/₂" x 4¹/₂" rectangles (A) and eight 2" x 2¹/₂" rectangles (D). Cut one 1¹/₂" x 42" strip. Cut into sixteen 1¹/₂" squares (C).

From the medium rose print, cut one 4¹/₂" x 42" strip. Cut into four 4¹/₂" squares (B).

From the tan small print, cut four 1¹/₂" x 2¹/₂" rectangles (E).

Sashing

From the sage green large print, cut four 1¹/₂" x 42" strips. Cut into six 1¹/₂" x 8¹/₂" strips for the vertical sashing and six 1¹/₂" x 12¹/₂" strips for the horizontal sashing.

From the medium rose print, cut nine 1¹/₂" squares.

Borders

From the dark mauve large print, cut three 1" x 42" strips. Cut into two 1" x 19¹/₂" strips for the side inner borders and two 1" x 28¹/₂" strips for the top and bottom inner borders.

From the yellow textured solid, cut three 1¹/₂" x 42" strips. Cut into two 1¹/₂" x 20¹/₂" strips for the side middle borders and two 1¹/₂" x 30¹/₂" strips for the top and bottom middle borders.

From the pink/olive floral print, cut four 3¹/₂" x 42" strips. Cut into two 3¹/₂" x 22¹/₂" strips for the side outer borders and two 3¹/₂" x 36¹/₂" strips for the top and bottom outer borders.

ASSEMBLY

1. Join cottage pieces A through J to make four blocks.

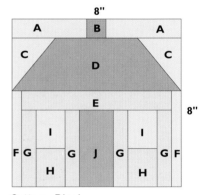

Cottage Block
Make 4

2. Join apple tree pieces A through D to make four blocks.

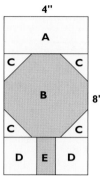

Apple Tree Block
Make 4

3. Stitch the Cottage and Apple Tree blocks together in pairs, with the tree to the right.

4. Lay out the units in two rows, as shown in the quilt photograph (page 143) and quilt diagram. Stitch the units together in rows, inserting vertical sashing strips in between and at each end. Press toward the sashing. Stitch the horizontal sashing strips and sashing squares together, making three strips as shown. Join the rows and horizontal sashing. Press.

5. Sew the side inner borders to the quilt top. Press. Add the top and bottom inner borders. Press. Follow the same sequence to add the side middle borders, top and bottom middle borders, side outer borders, and top and bottom outer borders, pressing after each addition.

6. Layer and finish the quilt. In *Emily's Cottage*, the patchwork shapes are quilted ¹/₄" from the edge.

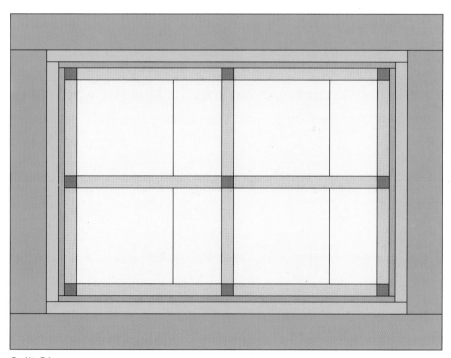

Quilt Diagram

Christmas Village

Designed by Jean Wells and Ursula Searles. Cottage block, 8";
House block, 8"; Pine Tree block, 4" x 8"; quilt size, 59" x 59"

Rows of houses and trees decorate this holiday scene. Try adapting the fabrics to depict the streets in your own neighborhood. The stars around the border are a bonus, especially when you piece them from scraps.

BASIC INSTRUCTIONS

House Block (page 134)
Cottage Block (page 135)
Pine Tree Block (page 136)
Straight Set (page 43)
Finishing a Quilt (page 46)

MATERIALS

$3^1/4$ yards total assorted red, green, blue, and white prints and plaids
$2^3/4$ yards off-white textured solid
$3/8$ yard red solid
$1/2$ yard green floral print
$1/8$ yard brown wood-grain print
$3/8$ yard for binding
$3^1/2$ yards backing
63" x 63" batting

CUTTING

House Blocks (10)

Prepare House templates C, D, and E (pages 138–139).

From the off-white, cut two $1^1/2$" x 42" strips. Cut into thirty $1^1/2$" x $2^1/2$" rectangles (A). Cut two 3" x 42" strips. Layer the strips right sides together, and cut 20 C through both layers, or 40 total (20 in reverse).

From the assorted plaids and prints, cut twenty $1^1/2$" squares (B), 10 D, 10 E, twenty $1^1/2$" x $4^1/2$" rectangles (F), twenty $1^3/4$" x 4" rectangles (G), ten 2" x 4" rectangles (H), twenty $1^1/2$" x $2^1/2$" rectangles (I), ten $2^1/2$" squares (J), and ten 2" x $4^1/2$" rectangles (K). Refer to the quilt photograph for color ideas. In this quilt, each house block uses matching fabrics for pieces G and F and for pieces F, I, and K. The chimneys are red plaid and the windows and doors are white or light in value.

Cottage Blocks (9)

Prepare Cottage templates C and D (page 138).

From the off-white, cut two $1^1/2$" x 42" strips. Cut into nine $1^1/2$" x $4^1/2$" rectangles (A1) and nine $1^1/2$" x $3^1/2$" rectangles (A2). Cut one 3" x 42" strip. Fold in half, right side in, and cut 9 C through both layers, or 18 total (nine in reverse). Cut one 5" x 19" strip. Cut into eighteen 5" x 1" rectangles (F).

From the assorted plaids and prints, cut nine $1^1/2$" squares (B), 9 D, nine $1^1/2$" x $7^1/2$" rectangles (E), eighteen $1^1/4$" x 4" rectangles (G), nine $1^3/4$" x $2^1/4$" rectangles (H), nine $1^3/4$" x $2^1/4$" rectangles (I), nine 2" x 4" rectangles (J), and nine $3^1/4$" x 4" rectangles (K). Refer to the quilt photograph for color ideas. In this quilt, each cottage block uses matching fabrics for pieces E, G, H, and K. The chimneys are dark red and the windows and doors are white or light in value.

Pine Tree Blocks (17)

Prepare Pine Tree templates A and B (pages 138–139).

From the off-white, cut three $7^1/2$" x 42" strips. Fold each strip in half, right side in, and cut 17 A through both layers, or 34 total (17 in reverse). Cut two 2" x 42" strips. Cut into forty 2" squares (C).

From various blue and green plaids and prints, cut 17 B.

From the brown wood-grain print, cut one 2" x 42" strip. Cut into seventeen 2" x $1^1/2$" rectangles (D).

Friendship Star Border Units (48)

From the assorted prints and plaids, cut 48 matching sets of one 2" square (A) and two $2^3/8$" squares for B.

From the off-white, cut six $2^3/8$" x 42" strips. Cut into ninety-six $2^3/8$" squares for B. Place the B squares right sides together in print/white and plaid/white pairs; cut diagonally in half for 192 layered half-square triangles (B, C). Do not separate the pairs; they are ready for sewing. From the off-white, also cut ten 2" x 42" strips. Cut into one hundred ninety-two 2" squares (D).

Spacers, Sashing, and Inner Border

From the off-white, cut one $8^{1}/_{2}$" x 42" strip. Cut into eight $8^{1}/_{2}$" x $1^{1}/_{2}$" rectangles and six $8^{1}/_{2}$" x $2^{1}/_{2}$" rectangles for the spacers.

From the green floral print, cut five $2^{1}/_{2}$" x 42" strips. Sew into one long strip. Cut into four $2^{1}/_{2}$" x $48^{1}/_{2}$" strips for the sashing.

From the red, cut five $1^{1}/_{4}$" x 42" strips. Sew into one long strip. Cut into two $1^{1}/_{4}$" x $48^{1}/_{2}$" strips for the side inner borders and two $1^{1}/_{4}$" x 50" strips for the top and bottom inner borders.

ASSEMBLY

1. Join house pieces A through K to make 10 blocks.

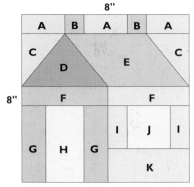

House Block
Make 10

2. Join cottage pieces A through K to make nine blocks. In this version of the block, there is one window, instead of two, and the chimney is off-center.

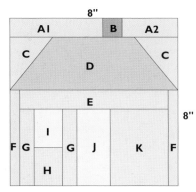

Cottage Block
Make 9

3. Join pine tree pieces A through D to make 17 blocks.

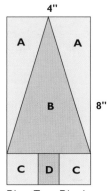

Pine Tree Block
Make 17

4. Chain-sew the B and C border triangles together as paired. Press open and trim off the ears. Arrange 1 A, 4 BC, and 4 D squares in three rows as shown, matching the A and B fabrics. Stitch the pieces together in rows. Press. Join the rows. Press. Make 48 units total.

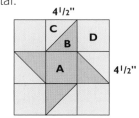

Friendship Star Unit
Make 48

5. Lay out the House, Cottage, and Pine Tree blocks and the $1^{1}/_{2}$" and $2^{1}/_{2}$" spacers in five rows, as shown in the quilt photograph (page 146) and quilt diagram. Stitch the pieces together in rows, pressing after each addition. Join the rows together, inserting the green floral print sashing strips in between for the lawn. Press.

6. Sew the side inner borders to the quilt top. Press. Add the top and bottom inner borders. Press. Stitch the star units together, making two strips of 11 stars each for the side outer borders and two strips of 13 stars each for the top and bottom outer borders. Join the borders to the quilt, pressing after each addition.

7. Layer and finish the quilt. *Christmas Village* was machine-quilted in-the-ditch between the blocks.

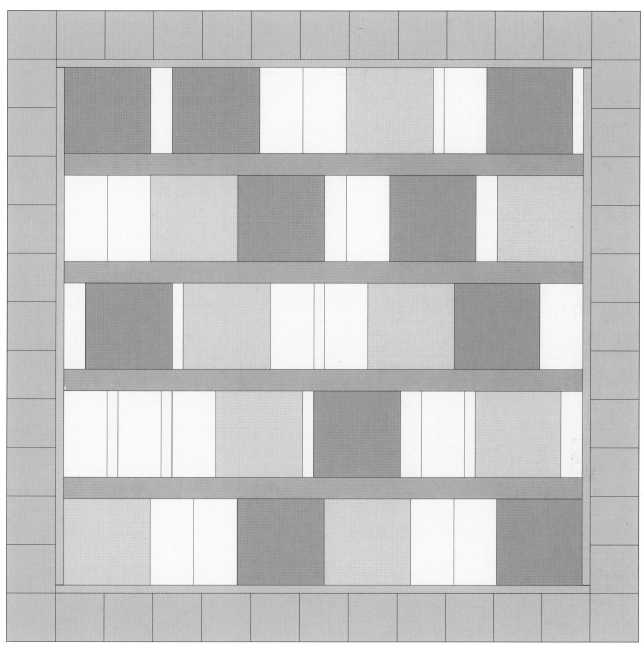

Quilt Diagram

House blocks

Cottage blocks

Pine Tree blocks

Friendship Star units

CHAPTER 8

Free-Form Piecing

*B*reak away from precision cutting with freestyle Crazy-Patch blocks. Then try your hand at curved piecing. This chapter's off-beat quilts will have you looking at your fabric stash in a whole new way.

CRAZY-PATCH

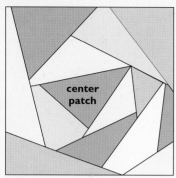

center patch

Block Diagram

Crazy-patch piecing got its start in a hand quilting craze of the late nineteenth century. Today's version is done by machine on a muslin foundation. Randomly shaped patches are placed right sides together on the foundation and stitched through all three layers. The top patch is flipped over to conceal the seam. Just keep adding more patches until the entire foundation is filled. It's the perfect technique for using up fabric odds and ends.

FOR AN 8" CRAZY-PATCH BLOCK:

Prepare the center triangle template (page 155). Cut the following pieces:

one center triangle

2"- to 3"-wide assorted strips or scraps

one 9" square of muslin

1. Place the irregular triangle right side up in the center of the muslin square.

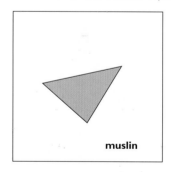

muslin

2. Place a strip (or scrap) on top, right sides together and matching along one edge. Stitch through all three layers using a ¹/₄" seam allowance.

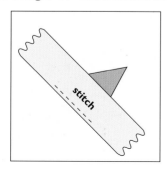

stitch

3. Flip the strip over the seam allowance and finger-press from the right side. Trim the strip to make a new shape.

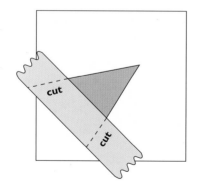

cut

cut

QUILTER'S TIP

Use the irregular center triangle in a Crazy-Patch block to show off a theme print or a special design.

4. Repeat steps 2 and 3, adding new pieces and building out from the center. Trim out any excess bulk. When the entire muslin foundation is covered, press from the right side. Use your rotary cutter and ruler to true up the block to 8¹/₂" square (for an 8" finished size).

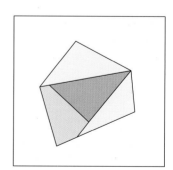

BASIC BLOCK CRAZY LOG CABIN

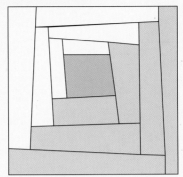

Block Diagram

This freestyle version of the Log Cabin block is the perfect exercise if you're trying to loosen up your piecing. Start by cutting a lopsided square, about 2" across, for the center patch. Build up the block with light and dark strips, as for a traditional Log Cabin, but deliberately skew the stitching lines for a quirky look.

FOR A 7" CRAZY LOG CABIN BLOCK:

Prepare the center patch template (page 155). Cut the following pieces:
  one light, medium, or bright lopsided square (use the template)
  2"- to 3"-wide strips, in assorted lights and darks
  one 8" square of muslin

▧ QUILTER'S TIP

Be picky when choosing a Crazy-Patch palette. The Crazy-Patch shapes may be uneven, but the rules of color and value still apply. Make sure your fabrics share a common mood or theme to give the block continuity.

1. Place the lopsided square right side up and slightly off-center on the muslin square.

2. Place a light strip on top of the lopsided square, right sides together and the right edges matching. Stitch through all three layers using a $1/4$" seam allowance.

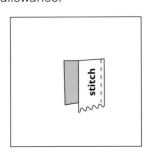

3. Flip the strip over the seam allowance and finger-press from the right side. Trim the outside edge of the strip at a slight angle. Even up the ends.

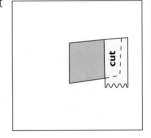

4. Rotate the block clockwise one quarter turn. Select a new light strip and repeat step 2.

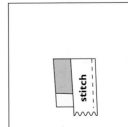

5. Flip, press, and trim the strip, as in step 3.

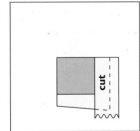

6. Repeat steps 4 and 5 two more times with dark strips to complete the first round. Add two more rounds. When the entire muslin foundation is covered, press from the right side. Using your rotary cutter and ruler, true up the block to $7^{1}/2$" square (for a 7" finished size).

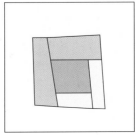

CURVED FAN

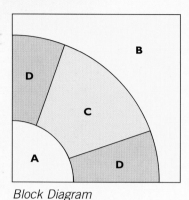

Block Diagram

The Curved Fan block will add a gentle arc to your piecing skills. There are two curved seams to sew. The tricky part is getting them to lie flat. Clipping into the seam allowance on the inside curve provides the ease that's required.

FOR A 6" FAN BLOCK:

Prepare templates A, B, C, and D (page 155). Cut the following pieces:

1 A	1 C
1 B	2 D

1. Stitch the D's to each side of C. Press toward C.

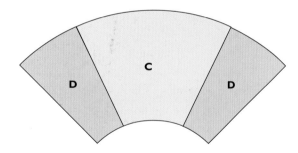

2. Using small sharp scissors, clip into the seam allowance along the inside curve of DCD. Make the clips $1/8$" deep and $1/4$" apart. Spacing the clips evenly will ensure a smooth curve.

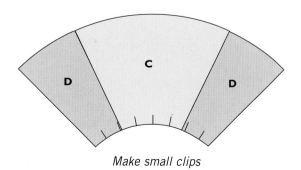

Make small clips

3. Use a pin to mark the midpoint of the clipped edge. Pin the curved edge of A to correspond. Place A and DCD right sides together, matching the midpoints. Pin together, and then remove the marker pins. Line up the straight edges at the sides and pin.

4. With DCD on top, stitch the curve $1/4$" from the raw edges. Go slowly, stitching about 1", and then stop. Adjust the fabric in front of the needle so that the raw edges are together, and then continue sewing. If you take it slowly and are careful, it will turn out perfectly!

5. Repeat step 2 to clip the inside curve of B. Repeat step 3 to pin B to DCD. Repeat step 4 to stitch the seam.

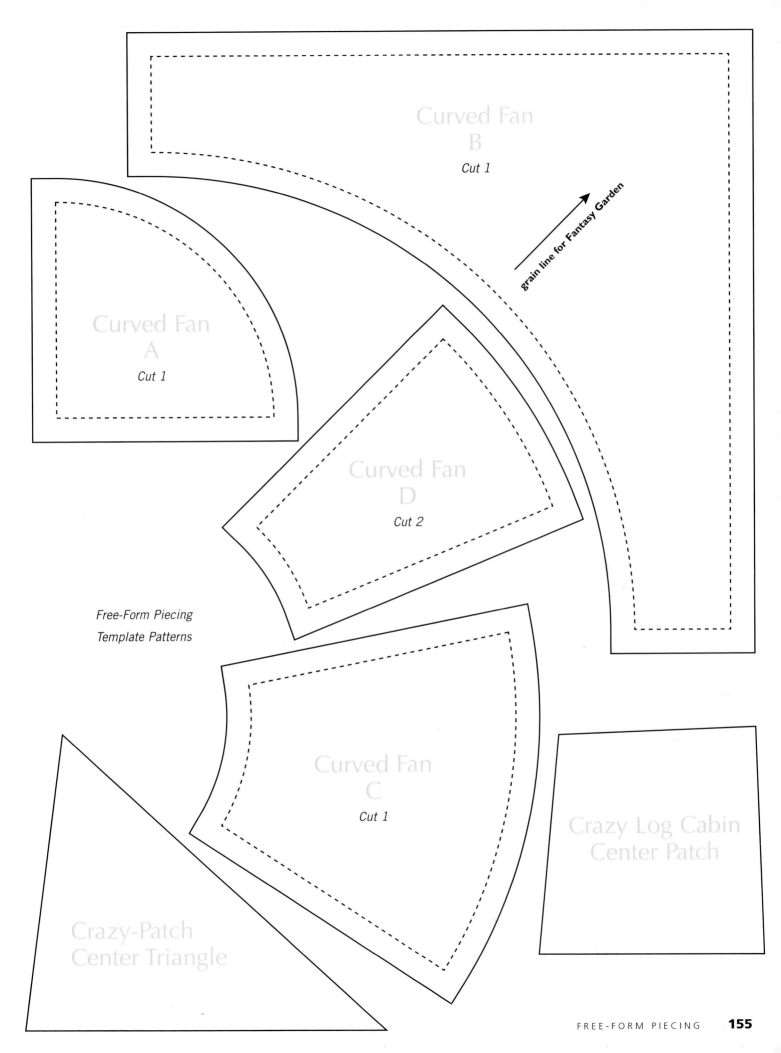

Curved Fan
B
Cut 1

grain line for Fantasy Garden

Curved Fan
A
Cut 1

Curved Fan
D
Cut 2

Free-Form Piecing
Template Patterns

Curved Fan
C
Cut 1

Crazy-Patch
Center Triangle

Crazy Log Cabin
Center Patch

In the Woods

Designed by Jean Wells. Block size, 8"; quilt size, 21¹/₄" x 21¹/₄".

F abrics with a mountain lodge look were chosen for this crazy-patch quilt. Pinecones, needled branches, bird nests, berries, and woodsy-colored plaids are some of the motifs and fabrics that mix together in these blocks. Deep green cotton velveteen brings plush warmth and texture to the sashing and border. Study each block for crazy-patch piecing ideas.

BASIC INSTRUCTIONS

Crazy-Patch Block (page 152)
Straight Set (page 43)
Finishing a Quilt (page 46)

MATERIALS

1¼ yards total assorted "woodsy" prints and plaids

¼ yard green cotton velveteen

¼ yard burgundy/green print for binding

¾ yard backing

¼ yard muslin

26" x 26" batting

CUTTING

Crazy-Patch Blocks (4)

Prepare the center triangle template (page 155).

From the woodsy prints and plaids, cut four triangles for the block centers, using the template. For variety, cut some of the triangles freehand, so that each piece is different. Look for interesting images or sections of the fabric to spotlight; see the quilt photograph for ideas. Cut the remaining prints and plaids into 2"- to 3"-wide strips.

From the muslin, cut four 9" squares.

Sashing

From the green velveteen, cut one 1¾" x 42" strip. Cut into two 1¾" x 8½" strips for the horizontal sashing and one 1¾" x 17¾" strip for the vertical sashing.

Border

From the green velveteen, cut two 2¼" x 42" strips. Cut each strip into one 2¼" x 17¾" strip for a top or bottom border and one 2¼" x 21¼" strip for a side border.

✹ QUILTER'S TIP

A crazy-patch block will be more interesting if the sides of the triangles are different lengths and the angles don't match. Keep this in mind as you trim the strips after sewing. If you are making multiple blocks, start with a different shape in the center each time.

ASSEMBLY

1. Use the muslin squares, the pre-cut triangles, and the assorted strips to make four Crazy-Patch blocks. Trim to 8½" square (for a finished block size of 8").

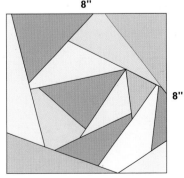

*Crazy-Patch Block
Make 4*

2. Lay out the blocks as shown, inserting the sashing strips in between. Stitch the blocks and horizontal sashing strips together in columns. Press. Join the columns and vertical sashing. Press.

3. Sew the top and bottom borders to the quilt top. Press. Add the side borders. Press.

4. Layer and finish the quilt. In-the-ditch stitching defines the sashing, block outlines, and selected crazy-patch shapes of *In the Woods*. The velveteen sashing and borders are left unquilted to avoid crushing the nap.

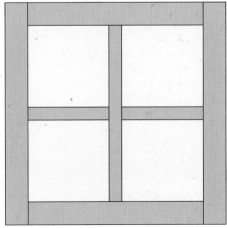

Quilt Diagram

Playful Sunshine

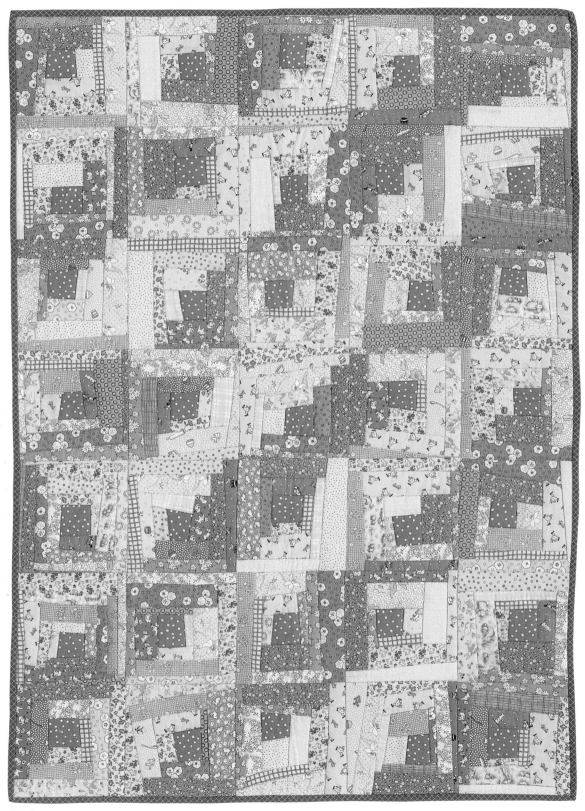

Designed by Jean Wells. Block size, 7"; quilt size, 35$^1/_2$" x 49$^1/_2$"

B lue and yellow 1930s-style prints make up the palette in this crazy-patch Log Cabin design. Use scraps of fabric, cut into short strips, to create the crazy-patch logs. Bits of red in the logs inspired the bright red binding, which acts as a narrow border.

BASIC INSTRUCTIONS

Crazy Log Cabin Block (page 153)
Straight Set (page 43)
Finishing a Quilt (page 46)

MATERIALS

1 yard total assorted yellow prints
1 yard total assorted blue prints
$^1/_4$ yard white-on-blue dotted print
$^1/_4$ yard red print for binding
$1^5/_8$ yards backing
$1^5/_8$ yards muslin
40" x 54" batting

CUTTING

Prepare the center patch template (page 155).

From the white-on-blue dotted print, cut three 3" x 42" strips. Use the template to cut 35 center patches, stacking the strips to speed the cutting. For variety, cut some of the patches freehand.

Cut the assorted blue and yellow prints into 2"- to 3"-wide strips.

From the muslin, cut seven 8" x 42" strips. Cut into thirty-five 8" squares.

ASSEMBLY

1. Use the muslin squares, the center patches, and the assorted yellow and blue strips to make 35 Crazy Log Cabin blocks. In each round, use yellow for strips 1 and 2 and blue for strips 3 and 4. Force yourself to cut the strips askew. For an extra-playful look, piece some blocks in a clockwise direction and some in a counterclockwise direction. Trim to $7^1/_2$" square (for a finished block size of 7").

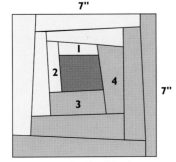

Crazy Log Cabin Block
Make 35

2. Lay out the blocks in seven rows of five blocks each. Rotate the blocks as shown in the quilt photograph and quilt diagram so that the yellow and blue strips create diagonal lines across the surface. Show your playfulness by turning one block askew.

3. Stitch the blocks together in rows. Press. Sew the rows together. Press.

4. Layer and finish the quilt. The piecing is so crazy in *Playful Sunshine*, it doesn't make sense to add more designs. The blocks are quilted in-the-ditch.

Quilt Diagram

House Party

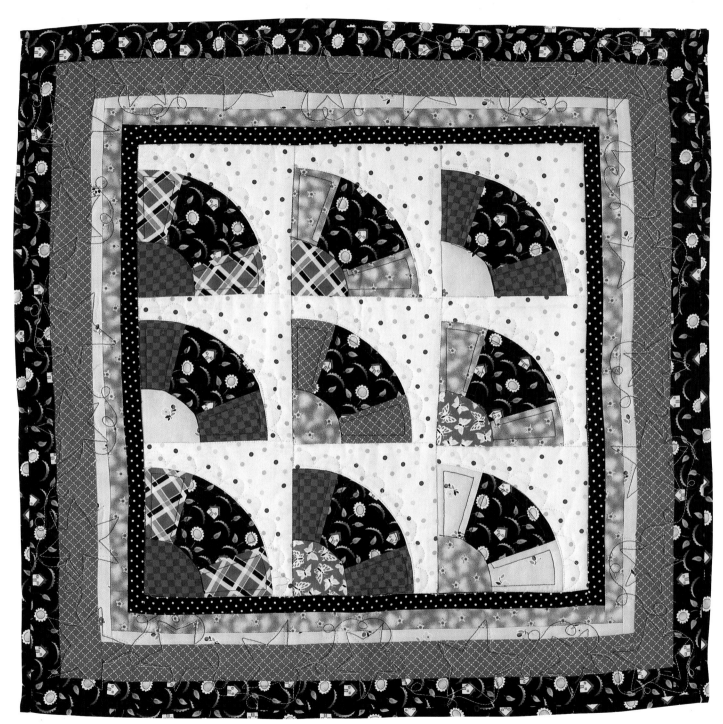

Designed by Jean Wells. Block size, 6"; quilt size, 28" x 28".

Bright primary colors show off the fans in this perky design. The black print provided the color inspiration. Multiple borders in different widths frame the diagonal block setting.

BASIC INSTRUCTIONS

Curved Fan Block (page 154)
Straight Set (page 43)
Finishing a Quilt (page 46)

MATERIALS

$1/2$ yard blue/yellow-on-white dotted print

$3/8$ yard red windowpane check

$3/8$ yard black print

$1/4$ yard yellow print

$1/4$ yard blue cloud print

$1/8$ yard cream-on-black dotted print

$1/8$ yard royal blue print

$1/8$ yard red plaid

$1/8$ yard red print

$1/4$ yard for binding

1 yard backing

32" x 32" batting

CUTTING

Curved Fan Blocks (9)

Prepare curved fan templates A, B, C, and D (page 155). Read the tip on page 164 and plan your cutting sequence.

From the assorted red, blue, and yellow fabrics, cut 9 A and 18 D. See the quilt photograph for color ideas.

From the blue/yellow-on-white dotted print, cut 9 B.

From the black print, cut 9 C.

Borders

From the cream-on-black dotted print, cut two $1^1/4$" x 42" strips. Cut into two $1^1/4$" x $18^1/2$" strips for side border E and two $1^1/4$" x 20" strips for top and bottom border E.

From the blue cloud print, cut two $1^1/4$" x 42" strips. Cut each strip into one $1^1/4$" x 20" strip for side border F and one $1^1/4$" x $21^1/2$" strip for top or bottom border F.

From the yellow print, cut three 1" x 42" strips. Sew into one long strip. Cut into two 1" x $21^1/2$" strips for side border G and two 1" x $22^1/2$" strips for top and bottom border G.

From the red windowpane check, cut three 2" x 42" strips. Sew into one long strip. Cut into two 2" x $22^1/2$" strips for side border H and two 2" x $25^1/2$" strips for top and bottom border H.

From the black print, cut three $1^3/4$" x 42" strips. Sew into one long strip. Cut into two $1^3/4$" x $25^1/2$" strips for side border I and two $1^3/4$" x 28" strips for top and bottom border I.

✖ QUILTER'S TIP

If a print has a direction, such as trees that "grow" only one way, consider buying extra fabric and cutting the side border strips on the lengthwise grain and the top and bottom border strips on the crosswise grain. That way, all the images will appear right side up when the quilt is assembled.

ASSEMBLY

1. Sew pieces A, B, C, and D together to make nine blocks. Make sure the C fabrics in each block match.

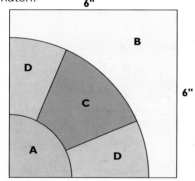

Curved Fan Block
Make 9 assorted

2. Lay out the blocks in three rows of three blocks each. Make sure patch A is in the lower left corner of each block, as shown in the quilt photograph. Stitch the blocks together in rows. Press. Join the rows together. Press.

3. Refer to the quilt diagram (page 162). Sew the E side borders to the quilt top. Press toward the border. Add the E top and bottom borders. Press. Add borders F, G, H, and I in the same sequence, pressing after each addition.

4. Layer and finish the quilt. In *House Party*, the fans are outline-quilted and a scalloped pattern fills in the background. A star motif is repeated around the border.

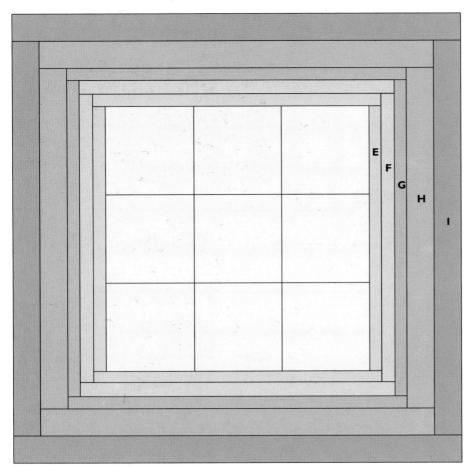

Quilt Diagram

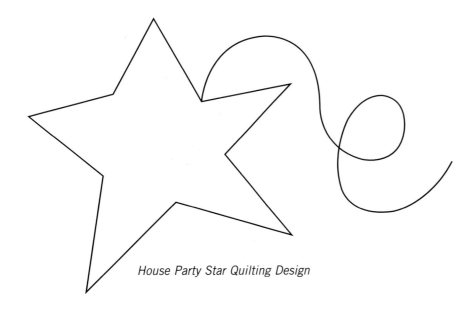

House Party Star Quilting Design

Fantasy Garden

Designed by Jean Wells. Block size, 6"; quilt size, 21¹/₂" x 21¹/₂".

Each fan shape in this quilted garden is filled in with crazy-patches for a unique, playful look. The curved seams are sewn in the usual way. In the background, a grassy print adds gentle undulating motion, as if tall vertical grasses were swaying in the breeze. To achieve this effect, place the background template at an angle when cutting the fabric.

BASIC INSTRUCTIONS

Crazy-Patch Block (page 152)
Curved Fan Block (page 154)
Diagonal Set (page 44)
Finishing a Quilt (page 46)

MATERIALS

$3/4$ yard total assorted pink, yellow, orange, and green floral prints and plaids
$3/8$ yard green/purple batik
$3/8$ yard red/green/purple plaid
$1/4$ yard pale green grass print
$1/8$ yard purple print
$1/4$ yard for binding
$3/4$ yard backing
$1/4$ yard muslin
26" x 26" batting

⊞ QUILTER'S TIP

When you are using the same fabrics for templates and a border, cut off the amount needed for the border at the beginning and set it aside. Then you can cut the smaller shapes without worrying whether your pattern layout will leave you short.

CUTTING

Crazy-Patch Fan Blocks (4)

Prepare Curved Fan templates A and B (page 155) and Crazy-Patch Fan template C (page 165). Read the tip (above) and plan your cutting sequence.
From the muslin, cut 4 C.
From the assorted prints and plaids, cut 4 A. You may wish to select the fabrics for these pieces after the crazy-patch fans are sewn.
From the pale green grass print, cut 4 B. Follow the grain line arrow on the template to create the tall grass effect shown in the quilt photograph (page 163).
From all the fabrics except the pale green grass print, cut 2"- to 3"-wide strips for crazy-patch. You may wish to select and cut these pieces as you sew.

Setting Triangles

From the green/purple batik, cut two $9^{3}/8$" squares; cut diagonally in half for four corner setting triangles.

Border

From the purple print, cut two 1" x 42" strips. Cut into four 1" x $12^{1}/2$" strips for the border accent.
From the red/green/purple plaid, cut two $2^{1}/2$" x 42" strips. Cut into four $2^{1}/2$" x $17^{1}/2$" strips for the side, top, and bottom borders.
From a yellow floral print, cut four $2^{1}/2$" squares for the border corners.

ASSEMBLY

1. Cut one of the crazy-patch fabrics into an uneven five- or six-sided shape. Place right side up in the middle of a muslin foundation C. Trim the edges even with the muslin.

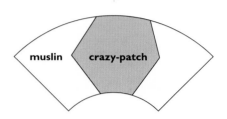

2. Use the crazy-patch piecing method to fill out the fan shape on one side. Be sure to choose contrasting fabrics for each patch. Trim even with the muslin.

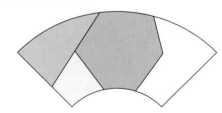

3. Repeat step 2 to fill out the other side.

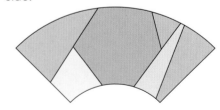

4. Stitch pieces A and B to each crazy-patch unit, using the curved seam technique. Repeat steps 1–4 to make four blocks total. Start with a different center shape each time and vary the fabrics so no two blocks are alike.

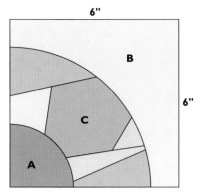

Crazy-Patch Fan Block
Make 4 assorted

6"

6"

5. Place the blocks on point, as shown in the quilt photograph (page 163) and quilt diagram. Stitch the blocks together in diagonal rows. Press. Join the rows. Press.

6. Fold each purple accent strip in half lengthwise, right side out, and press. Pin a strip to each edge of the four-block unit, raw edges matching. Overlap the ends at the corners. Place a corner setting triangle on top, right sides together and raw edges matching. Stitch through all the layers, trapping the accent strip in the seam. Fold the triangle over the seam and press from the right side. Add a triangle to the opposite edge. Press. Add triangles to the remaining edges. Press.

7. Sew the side borders to the quilt top. Press. Sew corner squares to the remaining border strips. Press. Join these strips to the top and bottom edges. Press.

8. Layer and finish the quilt. The individual crazy-patch shapes in *Fantasy Garden* are outline-quilted, calling attention to the fans. Stitching also defines and adds dimension to the long, flowing grasses, an outlining idea you can use with any printed fabric. In the border, straight stitching lines follow the plaid.

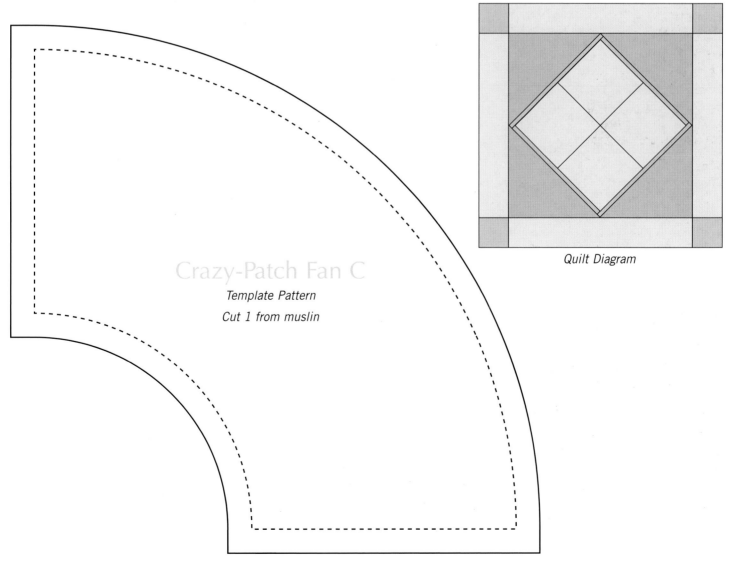

Crazy-Patch Fan C

Template Pattern

Cut 1 from muslin

Quilt Diagram

Appliqué

*A*ppliqués soften patchwork's strict geometry. Use appliqués to introduce curves, detailed shapes, or motifs from nature into your quilt designs. Add appliqués by hand, by machine, or by fusing.

CHAPTER 9

APPLIQUÉ **167**

DRESDEN PLATE

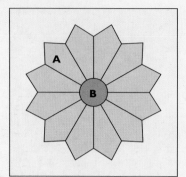

Block Diagram

Combine the prairie point look, piecing, and appliqué when you make the Dresden Plate block. Twelve wedges are stitched together in a ring and then hand-appliquéd to a background fabric. A circle appliqué conceals the raw edges at the center. Both plastic and freezer paper templates are used in this block, giving you a chance to try both template techniques.

FOR A 12" BLOCK:

Prepare plastic template A and freezer paper template B (page 172).

Cut the following pieces:

one $12^1/_2$" square

12 A wedges

1 B circle

1. Fold an A wedge lengthwise in half, right side in. Stitch across the broader end through both layers. Unfold the piece and lay it flat, forming a folded point at the seamed end. Lightly press the seam allowance open. Turn right side out, center the seam, and press flat to set the point. Make 12 wedges total.

Make 12

2. Arrange the wedges in a ring. Stitch the wedges right sides together in pairs, sewing from the broad end to the narrow end. Leave the points free. Press the seams open.

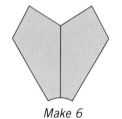

stitch

Make 6

3. Stitch the pairs together in groups of three, following your step 2 arrangement. Press. Sew the two halves together to complete the ring. Press.

4. Center the ring on the background square, right sides up. Pin in place. Hand-appliqué the outside pointed edge to the background square (see page 41 for instructions).

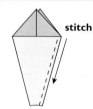

5. Center piece B (with its freezer paper template) on the wedge ring, concealing the ring's raw edges. Pin if desired. Hand-appliqué B in place, using your needle to turn under the fabric just beyond the edge of the template, for a smooth curve all around.

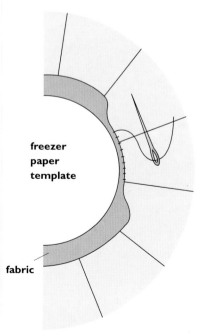

freezer paper template

fabric

BASIC BLOCK BUNNY

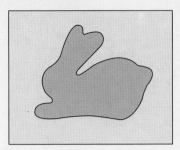

Block Diagram

The fused bunny appliqué is made just like the heart appliqué on page 42. To finish the edges, use a machine zigzag stitch or work buttonhole stitch by hand. Extend the same stitching within the appliqué to define the bunny's ear and hind leg. Note that the bunny design flip-flops during the fusing process, so that the finished appliqué is the reverse of the pattern you started out with.

FOR A 6" X 10" BLOCK, you will need:

one 6^1/$_2$" x 10^1/$_2$" rectangle

scrap, at least 6" x 10", for appliqué

paper-backed fusible webbing

1. Trace the small bunny pattern (page 179) onto the paper-backed side of the fusible web. Cut out the bunny shape about ^{1}/$_4$" beyond the marked line.

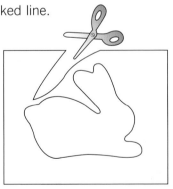

2. Lay the appliqué fabric right side down on the ironing board. Place the bunny cutout, web side down, on the fabric. Fuse in place, following the manufacturer's instructions.

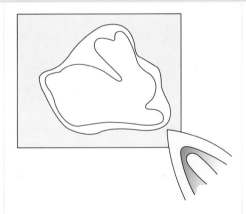

3. For easier handling, rough-cut the shape. Then cut out the bunny appliqué on the marked line.

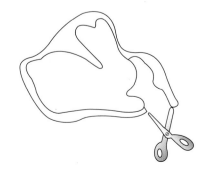

4. Peel off the paper backing. Lay the background fabric right side up. Position the appliqué right side up on top, and fuse in place.

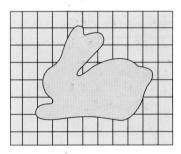

5. Work a closely spaced machine zigzag or a hand buttonhole stitch around the edges of the appliqué.

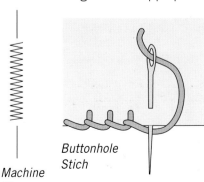

Machine Zigzag

Buttonhole Stich

Petal Play

Designed by Jean Wells. Block size, 12"; quilt size, 86 1/2" x 86 1/2".

T wo dozen springlike floral prints went into these Dresden Plate blocks. After cutting out the wedges, I rearranged them into various combinations. *Petal Play* reminds me of a meadow of wildflowers on a sunshiny day. With colors this bright, it's especially important to include green—nature's neutral—in the palette.

BASIC INSTRUCTIONS

Dresden Plate Block (page 168)
Straight Set (page 43)
Finishing a Quilt (page 46)

MATERIALS

$3^1/4$ yards light blue textured solid
$2^1/2$ yards pink/green floral print
$2^3/8$ yards total assorted floral prints
$1^1/4$ yards light green textured solid
$^3/8$ yard yellow textured solid
$^1/4$ yard coral textured solid
$^1/2$ yard for binding
$7^3/4$ yards backing
91" x 91" batting

CUTTING

Dresden Plate Blocks (25)

Prepare plastic template A and 25 freezer paper templates B (page 172).

From the assorted floral prints, cut 300 A. For more efficiency, stack up to four fabrics and cut multiples.

From the coral textured solid, cut 25 B. Remember to cut $^1/4$" beyond the edge of the freezer paper template.

From the light blue textured solid, cut nine $12^1/2$" x 42" strips. Cut into twenty-five $12^1/2$" squares.

Sashing

From the light green textured solid, cut fourteen $1^1/2$" x 42" strips. Cut into forty $1^1/2$" x $12^1/2$" strips.

From the yellow textured solid, cut one $1^1/2$" x 42" strip. Cut into sixteen $1^1/2$" squares.

Borders

From the light green textured solid, cut seven $1^1/2$" x 42" strips. Sew into one long strip. Cut into two $1^1/2$" x $64^1/2$" strips for the side inner borders and two $1^1/2$" x $66^1/2$" strips for the top and bottom inner borders.

From the yellow textured solid, cut seven 1" x 42" strips. Sew into one long strip. Cut into four 1" x $64^1/2$" strips for the border accents.

From the pink/green floral print, cut *on the lengthwise grain* two $10^1/2$" x $66^1/2$" strips for the side borders and two $10^1/2$" x $86^1/2$" strips for the top and bottom borders.

ASSEMBLY

1. Organize the A wedges into 25 groups of 12 pieces each, choosing a theme fabric and two or three companions for each group. Using one A group, one B circle, and one background square for each block, make 25 Dresden Plate blocks.

2. Lay out the blocks in five rows of five blocks each, as shown in the quilt photograph and quilt diagram (page 172). Stitch the blocks together in rows, inserting vertical sashing strips in between. Press toward the sashing. Stitch the horizontal sashing strips and squares together, making four horizontal strips as shown. Press toward the sashing. Join the rows and horizontal sashing. Press.

3. Sew the side inner borders to the quilt top. Press. Add the top and bottom inner borders. Press.

✖ QUILTER'S TIP

Template plastic comes in several thicknesses. I like the medium weight that is opaque. It does not slip as much as the clear template material. I choose a thickness that I can cut through with scissors.

Dresden Plate Block
Make 25

4. Fold each yellow accent strip lengthwise in half, right side out, and press. Pin a strip to each side edge of the quilt top, raw edges matching. Pin strips to the top and bottom edges, letting the strip ends overlap at the corners.

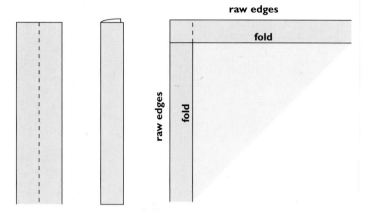

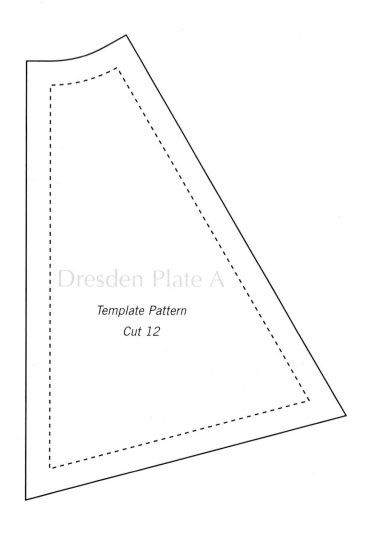

Quilt Diagram

5. Sew the side outside borders to the quilt, trapping the accent strips in the seams. On the right side, fold the border over the seam and press. Add the top and bottom borders and press in the same way.

6. Layer and finish the quilt. The Dresden Plate appliqués in *Petal Play* are quilted in the traditional way—$1/4$" from the edge—and the entire block is outlined. Stitching also accentuates the large floral pattern in the border.

Dresden Plate B

Template Pattern
Cut 1 from freezer paper

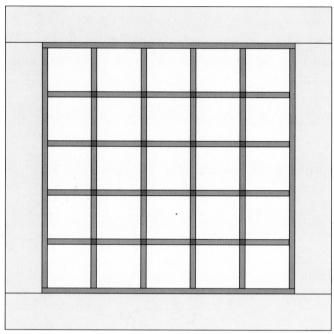

Dresden Plate A

Template Pattern
Cut 12

Bow Tie Fans

Designed by Jean Wells. Block size, 9$\frac{1}{2}$"; quilt size, 74$\frac{1}{2}$" x 93$\frac{1}{2}$".

F ans with pointed tips are assembled the same way as a Dresden Plate block. The fan wedges were cut from a collection of nostalgic prints and placed against a toile background. Two diagonally facing blocks form each bow tie in this interesting and compact setting.

BASIC INSTRUCTIONS

Dresden Plate Block (page 168)
Straight Set (page 43)
Finishing a Quilt (page 46)

MATERIALS

5 yards total assorted brown, green, and burgundy floral prints
$4^5/8$ yards ecru toile
1 yard sage green textured solid
1 yard sage green print
$^1/2$ yard light purple
$^1/2$ yard for binding
$5^1/2$ yards backing
79" x 98" batting

CUTTING

Bow Tie Fan Blocks (63)

Make plastic template A and 63 freezer paper templates B (page 175).

From the assorted floral prints, cut 378 A. For more efficiency, stack up to four fabrics and cut multiples.

From the sage green textured solid, cut 63 B. The template includes a $^1/4$" seam allowance.

From the ecru toile, cut sixteen 10" x 42" strips. Cut into sixty-three 10" squares.

Borders

From the light purple, cut eight $1^1/2$" x 42" strips. Sew into one long strip. Cut into two $1^1/2$" x 86" strips for the side inner borders and two $1^1/2$" x 69" strips for the top and bottom inner borders.

From the sage green print, cut nine $3^1/4$" x 42" strips. Sew into one long strip. Cut into two $3^1/4$" x 88" strips for the side outer borders and two $3^1/4$" x $74^1/2$" strips for the top and bottom outer borders.

ASSEMBLY

Refer to the Dresden Plate block instructions steps 1–3 (page 168).

1. Make a point at the broad end of each A wedge. Organize the A wedges into 63 groups of six pieces each. Stitch the wedges together in pairs, and then join three pairs.

2. Place a six-wedge fan on a toile square, right sides up and straight raw edges matching. Pin. Appliqué the pointed edge of the fan. Place piece B on the corner of the block, at the base of the fan. Turn under and appliqué the curved edge only. Make 63 fan blocks total.

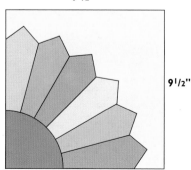

9½"

9½"

Fan Block
Make 63

3. Lay out the blocks in nine rows of seven blocks each, as shown in the quilt diagram. Rotate the blocks as shown in the quilt photograph (page 173) to create the bow tie pattern. Stitch the blocks together in rows. Press. Join the rows. Press.

4. Sew the side inner borders to the quilt top. Press. Add the top and bottom inner borders. Press. Add the side outer borders. Press. Add the top and bottom outer borders. Press.

5. Layer and finish the quilt. In keeping with *Bow Tie Fans'* traditional look, the fans were outline-quilted and a scroll design (page 175) appears in the open areas above them. A leaf motif was quilted in the border.

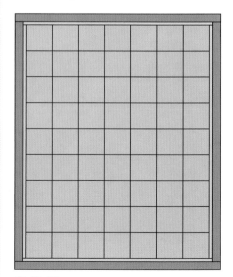

Quilt Diagram

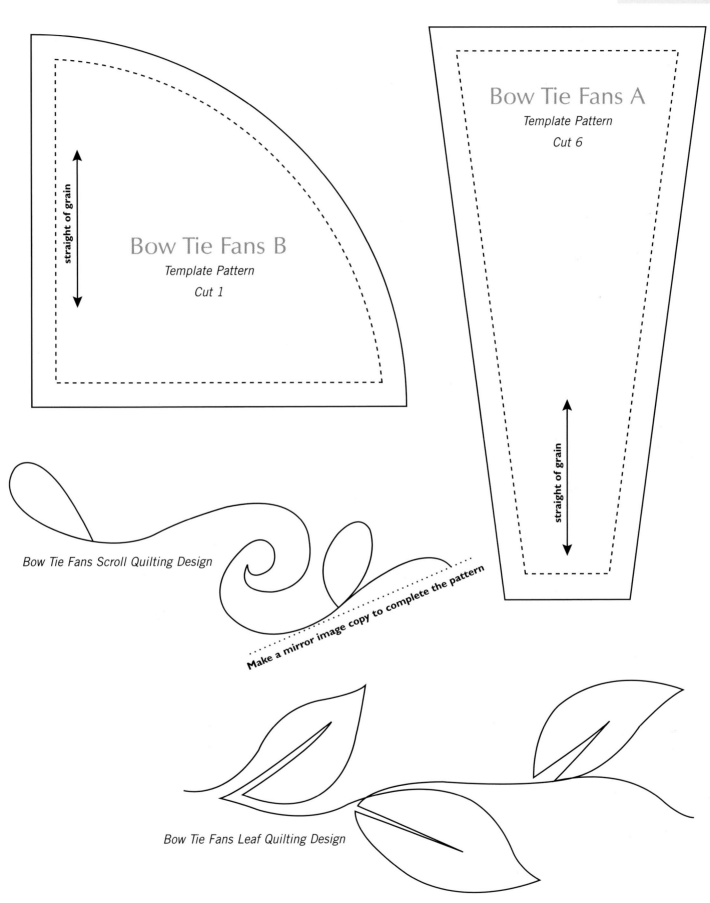

Bow Tie Fans B
Template Pattern
Cut 1

straight of grain

Bow Tie Fans A
Template Pattern
Cut 6

straight of grain

Bow Tie Fans Scroll Quilting Design

Make a mirror image copy to complete the pattern

Bow Tie Fans Leaf Quilting Design

Bunny Melody

Designed by Jean Wells. Pinwheel block size, 4"; Heart block size, 4"; quilt size, 35¹/₂" x 48¹/₂".

With its pinwheels, checkerboard frame, and appliquéd designs, *Bunny Melody* could almost be called a sampler quilt. The bunnies and hearts are needleturn-appliquéd, but they could easily be fused in place and buttonhole-stitched instead.

BASIC INSTRUCTIONS

Pinwheel Block (page 69)
Bunny Block (page 169)
Hand Appliqué (page 41)
Straight Set (page 43)
Finishing a Quilt (page 46)

MATERIALS

$7/8$ yard white solid
$5/8$ yard purple check
$1/2$ yard pale yellow print
Small prints:
  $1/2$ yard green
  $1/2$ yard lavender
  $1/2$ yard golden yellow
  $1/2$ yard blue
$1/8$ yard light green print
$1/4$ yard for binding
$1^1/2$ yards backing
39" x 53" batting

CUTTING

Pinwheel Blocks (14)

From the purple check and the small prints, cut one $2^7/8$" x 42" strip each, or five strips total. Cut each strip in half. Layer the strips right sides together in pairs, making five different combinations. Cut into 28 layered $2^7/8$" squares; cut diagonally in half for 56 layered triangles. Do not separate the pairs; they are ready for sewing.

Heart Blocks (6)

Prepare ten freezer paper heart templates (page 179).
From the purple check and the small prints, cut ten heart appliqués.
From the white solid, cut one $4^1/2$" x 42" strip; cut into six $4^1/2$" squares.

Bunny Panels

Prepare ten freezer paper bunny templates (reverse five) (page 179).
From the purple check and the small prints, cut ten bunny appliqués.
From the white solid, cut three 7" x 42" strips. Cut into one 7" x $18^1/2$" rectangle (A1) and two 7" x $27^1/2$" rectangles (B).
From the light green print, cut one 4" x 42" strip. Cut into one 4" x $18^1/2$" rectangle (A2).

Borders

From the golden yellow and lavender small prints, cut one $2^1/2$" x 42" strip each. Cut two $2^1/2$" squares from each strip. Leave the rest of the strips long.
From the pale yellow print, cut two $1^1/2$" x 42" strips. Sew into one long strip. Cut into two $1^1/2$" x $14^1/2$" strips for the side inner borders and two $1^1/2$" x $24^1/2$" strips for the top and bottom inner borders.
From the purple check, cut three 2" x 42" strips. Sew into one long strip. Cut into two 2" x $24^1/2$" strips for the side middle borders and two 2" x $27^1/2$" strips for the top and bottom middle borders.

From the pale yellow print, cut three $4^1/2$" x 42" strips. Cut into four $4^1/2$" x $18^1/2$" rectangles (C) for the side outer borders and four $4^1/2$" x 12" rectangles (D) for the top and bottom outer borders.

✜ QUILTER'S TIP

There are several ways to make a reverse pattern. If the pattern is not very complicated, simply trace it on tracing paper and then turn the tracing over. Go over the design lines to darken them. For more complex patterns, use a photocopier set for mirror image.

ASSEMBLY

1. Stitch the triangles together as paired. Join the units together in random groups of four to make 14 Pinwheel blocks. The pinwheel design may or may not be noticeable, depending on how the colors and values fall.

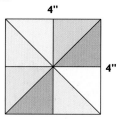

Pinwheel Block
Make 14 assorted

2. Hand-appliqué a heart to each white background square. Make 6 blocks total.

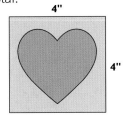

Heart Block
Make 6

3. Sew A1 and A2 together along one long edge, using a $^1/_4$" seam allowance. Press toward the green fabric. Stitch the golden yellow and lavender strips together. Press. Cut into $2^1/_2$" segments. Join the segments and the extra single squares to make two 1x5 checkerboard strips (lavender at each end) and two 1x11 checkerboard strips (golden yellow at each end). Stitch the 1x5 strips to the sides of panel A. Press toward the panel. Stitch the 1x11 checkerboard strips to the top and bottom edges. Press.

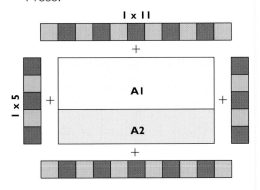

4. Lay the panel right side up, with the green "grass" at the bottom. Position two mirror image bunnies on the seam line and a heart appliqué in between, as shown in the quilt photograph (page 176). Hand-appliqué each piece in place. Lay out and appliqué four bunnies and two hearts to each B rectangle.

5. Add the side inner borders to the bunny unit. Press. Add the top and bottom inner borders. Press. Lay out three Pinwheel blocks and three appliquéd heart blocks in a row across the top edge of the unit, as shown in the quilt diagram. Arrange a second row across the bottom edge. Stitch the blocks together in rows. Press. Join each row to the unit. Press.

6. Add the side middle borders to the unit. Press. Add the top and bottom middle borders. Press. Add the B bunny panels to the top and bottom edges. Press.

7. Stitch 2 C's to a Pinwheel block for each side outer border. Press toward C. Stitch 2 D's and three Pinwheel blocks together for the top and bottom borders. Press toward D. Add the side outer borders to the quilt top. Press. Add the top and bottom outer borders. Press.

Bunny Melody Daisy
Quilting Design

daisy petal
repeat

To extend this pattern,
draw a gentle wavy line
and add petal shapes.

Bunny Melody Scallop Quilting Design

8. Layer and finish the quilt. In *Bunny Melody*, the pieced shapes and appliqués are outline-quilted. The scalloped design in the border was made by sketching a graceful curve and adding petal shapes along one edge. Creating this type of design to fit a specific area is easy since the shapes don't have to be exactly alike. One of the fabric prints inspired the daisies quilted in the lawn.

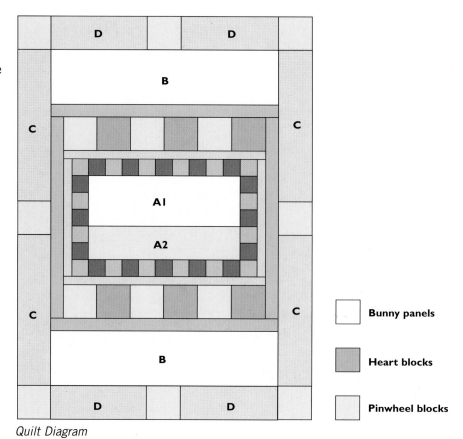

Quilt Diagram

☐ **Bunny panels**

■ **Heart blocks**

☐ **Pinwheel blocks**

Small Bunny

Template Pattern

Make 10 (reverse 5)

topstitching

topstitching

Heart

Template Pattern

Make 10

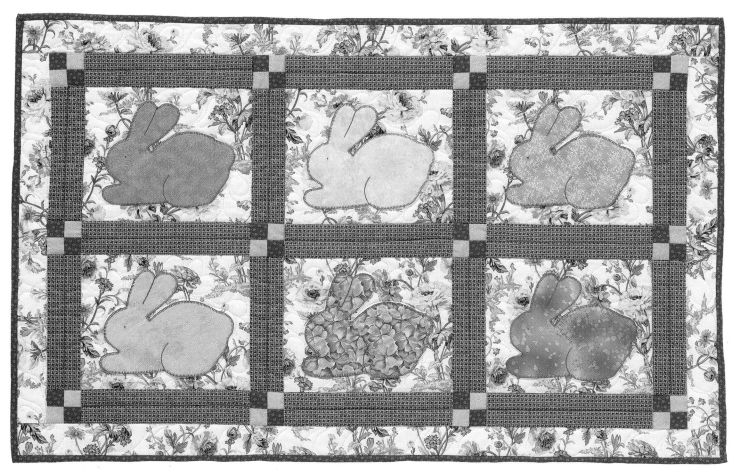

Designed by Jean Wells. Block size, 8" x 10"; quilt size, 26$\frac{1}{2}$" x 42$\frac{1}{2}$".

Bunnies with buttonhole-stitched edges play in a flowery meadow. Sashing and checkerboard squares impose a grid on the design and make each bunny seem more special.

BASIC INSTRUCTIONS

Bunny Block (page 169)
Fusible Appliqué (page 42)
Straight Set (page 43)
Finishing a Quilt (page 46)

MATERIALS

⁷/₈ yard large floral print

¹/₂ yard olive textured solid

¹/₈ yard brick red textured solid

¹/₈ yard tan

scraps of pink, lavender, and golden tan

¹/₄ yard for binding

1³/₈ yards backing

31" x 47" batting

embroidery floss

paper-backed fusible web

CUTTING

Bunny Blocks (6)

Use the bunny pattern (page 183) and the pink, lavender, and golden tan scraps to prepare six fusible appliqués.

From the large floral print, cut two 8¹/₂" x 42" strips. Cut into six 8 ¹/₂" x 10¹/₂" rectangles for the block backgrounds.

Sashing

From the olive textured solid, cut five 2¹/₂" x 42" strips. Cut into eight 2¹/₂" x 8¹/₂" strips for the vertical sashing and nine 2¹/₂" x 10¹/₂" strips for the horizontal sashing.

From the brick red and the tan, cut one 1¹/₂" x 42" strip each.

Border

From the large floral print, cut four 2¹/₂" x 42" strips. Sew into one long strip. Cut into two 2¹/₂" x 22¹/₂" strips for the side outer borders and two 2¹/₂" x 42¹/₂" strips for the top and bottom outer borders.

ASSEMBLY

1. Fuse the bunny appliqués to the background blocks. Work buttonhole stitch in two strands of floss around the edges and on the design lines marked on the pattern, to define the ears and hind legs.

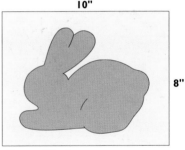

Bunny Block
Make 6

2. Stitch the brick red and tan strips together. Press. Cut into twenty-four 1¹/₂" segments. Stitch the segments together in pairs to make 12 Four-Patch units.

Four-Patch Unit
Make 12

3. Lay out the Bunny blocks in two rows of three blocks each, as shown in the quilt photograph and quilt diagram (page 182). Join the blocks together in rows, inserting vertical sashing strips in between and at each end. Stitch the horizontal sashing strips and Four-Patch units together to make three long horizontal sashing strips. Join the bunny rows and horizontal sashing strips as shown. Press.

4. Add the side outer borders to the quilt top. Press. Add the top and bottom outer borders. Press.

5. Layer and finish the quilt. Each bunny appliqué in *Rabbit Patch* is outline-stitched and surrounded by quilted swirls, giving the effect that the bunny is resting in a bed of flowers. Straight quilting lines appear in the sashing.

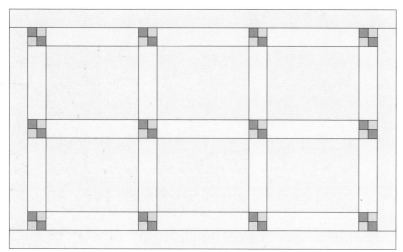

Quilt Diagram

Bunny Fusible Appliqué

Make 6

Quilting Design (in reverse)

Sampler Quilts

Sampler quilts provide continuous fascination. Each block you make offers new piecing combinations—and the opportunity to use up some of those scraps you've been saving. Work out a color palette, and then have fun creating all of your favorite blocks.

Forest Sampler

Designed by Jean Wells. Block size, 12"; quilt size, 37³/₄" x 37³/₄".

A print with forest animals inspired this four-block sampler. This project teaches all the basics of quiltmaking, from strip piecing to appliqué. It has a little bit of everything yet isn't too large. Look how a little gold fabric mixed in creates an underlying glow.

BASIC INSTRUCTIONS

Blocks (in alphabetical order)
   Aunt Vina's Favorite (page 106)
   House (page 134)
   Nine-Patch (page 52)
   Pine Tree (page 137)
   Sawtooth Star (page 88)
Hand Appliqué (page 41)
Straight Set (page 43)
Finishing a Quilt (page 46)

MATERIALS

1 yard animal theme print
$1/2$ yard black solid
Hand-dyed solids:
   $1/4$ yard brick red
   $1/4$ yard blue
   $3/8$ yard yellow
   $3/8$ yard gold
Small ethnic prints:
   $1/4$ yard yellow
   $1/4$ yard olive/brown
   $1/4$ yard orange
   $1/8$ yard brown
   $1/8$ yard black/brown
$1/4$ yard for binding
$1 1/4$ yards backing
42" x 42" batting

CUTTING

Block 1: Aunt Vina's Favorite

Follow the 12" block cutting guide on page 106.

From the animal theme print, cut 1 A.
From the blue hand-dyed solid, cut 4 B and 4 E.
From the gold hand-dyed solid, cut 4 C.
From the yellow hand-dyed solid, cut 8 D.
From the brick red hand-dyed solid, cut 16 F.

Block 2: Pinebrook

Follow the 8" House block cutting guide on page 134. Prepare templates C, D, and E (pages 138–139).
From the yellow hand-dyed solid, cut 3 A, 2 C (reverse one), and 1 J.
From the orange ethnic print, cut 2 B.
From the brick red hand-dyed solid, cut 1 D, 2 F, 2 G, 2 I, and 1 K.
From the black/brown ethnic print, cut 1 E and one $1 1/2$" x $12 1/2$" strip for the fence.
From the gold hand-dyed solid, cut 1 H.
Follow the 4" x 8" Pine Tree block cutting guide on page 136. Prepare templates A and B (pages 138–139).
From the yellow hand-dyed solid, cut 2 A (reverse one) and 2 C.
From the olive/brown ethnic print, cut 1 B and one $3 1/2$" x $12 1/2$" strip for the lawn.
From a brown section of the animal theme print, cut 1 D.

Block 3: Nine-Patch and Appliqué

Use the tree pattern on page 189 to make two freezer paper templates.
From the olive/brown ethnic print, cut two tree appliqués.
From the yellow ethnic print, cut two $6 1/2$" squares.
From the remaining ethnic prints and hand-dyed solids, cut 18 assorted $2 1/2$" squares.

Block 4: Sawtooth Star

Follow the 12" block cutting guide on page 88.
From the animal theme print, cut 1 A and 8 B.
From the gold hand-dyed solid, cut 4 C and 4 D.

Sashing and Borders

From the black solid, cut six $2 1/4$" x 42" strips. Cut into two $2 1/4$" x $12 1/2$" strips for the horizontal sashing, three $2 1/4$" x $26 1/4$" strips for the vertical sashing and the side inner borders, and two $2 1/4$" x $29 3/4$" strips for the top and bottom inner borders.
From the orange ethnic print, cut four $1 1/2$" x 42" strips. Cut into two $1 1/2$" x $29 3/4$" strips for the side middle borders and two $1 1/2$" x $31 3/4$" strips for the top and bottom middle borders.
From the animal theme print, cut *on the lengthwise grain* two $3 1/2$" x $31 3/4$" strips for the side outer borders. From the remaining fabric, cut on the crosswise grain three $3 1/2$" x 35" strips. Sew into one long strip. Cut into two $3 1/2$" x $37 3/4$" strips for the top and bottom outer borders.

ASSEMBLY

Refer to the Basic Block instructions to assemble blocks 1–4.

1. Make one Aunt Vina's Favorite block.

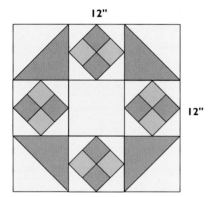

Block 1: Aunt Vina's Favorite

2. Make one 8" House block and one 4" x 8" Pine Tree block. Stitch the blocks together as shown. Press. Sew the fence strip to the bottom edge. Press. Add the grass strip. Press.

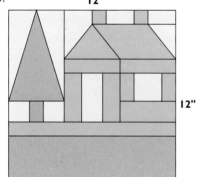

Block 2: Pinebrook

3. Needleturn-appliqué a tree to each 6$\frac{1}{2}$" yellow square. Sew the 2$\frac{1}{2}$" squares together to make two Nine-Patch units. Lay out the pieces in a Four-Patch as shown. Stitch together in rows. Press. Join the rows. Press.

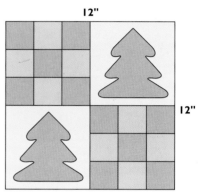

Block 3: Nine-Patch and Appliqué

4. Make one Sawtooth Star block.

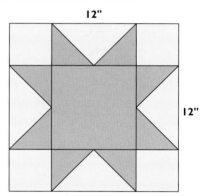

Block 4: Sawtooth Star

5. Lay out the four blocks as shown in the quilt photograph (page 186) and quilt diagram. Sew the blocks together in columns, inserting horizontal sashing strips in between. Press. Join the columns, inserting a vertical sashing strip in between. Press. Add the side inner borders. Press. Add the top and bottom inner borders. Press. Add the middle and outer borders in the same sequence, pressing after each addition.

6. Layer and finish the quilt. In *Forest Sampler*, the main shapes in each block are outline-quilted. The appliquéd tree reappears as a quilting design in the border. Quilted diamonds decorate the sashing.

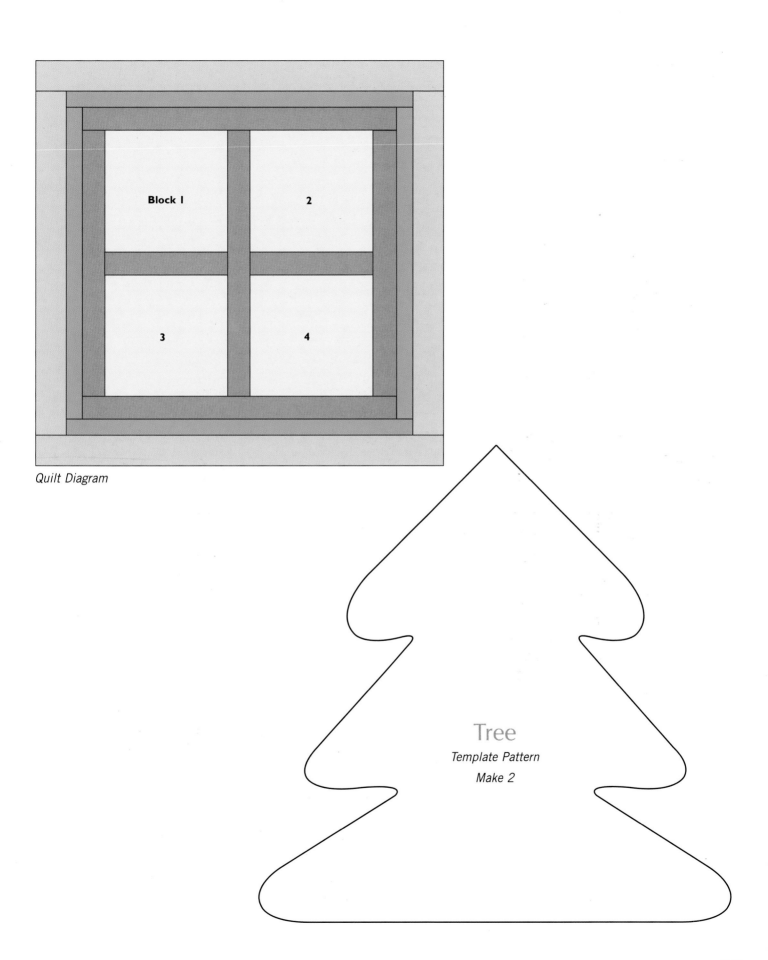

Quilt Diagram

Block 1   2

3   4

Tree
Template Pattern
Make 2

Heirloom Rose

Designed by Jean Wells. Block size, 12"; quilt size, 62³/4" x 77".

Antique quilts that combine brown, cream, and pink fabrics are among my favorites. This setting showcases all of the blocks featured in this book. If you study the quilt closely, you'll see how an individual fabric can take on different roles from block to block. The three-piece sashing calls extra attention to each block, much like a frame and mat around a piece of artwork. Repeat the sashing accent color in the binding to complete the effect.

MATERIALS

1¾ yards pink-on-cream floral print

⅞ yard brown solid

⅝ yard brown theme print

Assorted prints, plaids, and textured solids:

1½ yards total lights

1½ yards total mediums

1½ yards total darks

½ yard brown solid for binding

3⅞ yards backing

⅝ yard muslin

67" x 81" batting

CUTTING

Cut the pieces for each block, using the theme print, the coordinating fabrics, and, occasionally, the pink-on-cream print. Refer to the quilt photograph for ideas on how to combine different colors and fabric designs.

Block 1: Fruit Basket

Follow the 12" block cutting guide on page 119.

From a dark fabric, cut 1 A and 2 G.

From a light fabric, cut 1 B, 6 D, 1 E, 2 F, and 1 H.

From a medium fabric, cut 6 C.

Block 2: Log Cabin

Follow the 6" block cutting guide on page 53.

From a medium fabric, cut 4 A.

From a light fabric, cut 4 B and 4 C.

From a dark fabric, cut 4 D and 4 E.

From a light fabric, cut 4 F and 4 G.

From a dark fabric, cut 4 H and 4 I.

From a light fabric, cut 4 J and 4 K.

From the theme print, cut 4 L and 4 M.

Block 3: Dresden Plate

Follow the 12" block cutting guide on page 168. Prepare plastic template A and freezer paper template B (page 172).

From a light fabric, cut one 12½" square.

From two medium and two dark fabrics, cut 3 A each, for 12 total, and 1 B.

Block 4: Dolley Madison Star

Follow the 12" block cutting guide on page 172.

From the theme print, cut 5 A.

From a medium or light fabric, cut 4 B, 8 D, and 4 E.

From a dark fabric, cut 8 C.

Block 5: Flying Geese

Follow the 4" x 2" unit cutting guide on page 87.

From the assorted fabrics, cut 18 A and 36 B.

Block 6: Pinebrook

Follow the 8" House block cutting guide on page 134. Prepare templates C, D, and E (pages 138–139).

From a light fabric, cut 3 A and 2 C (reverse one).

From a dark fabric, cut 2 B.

From a dark fabric, cut 1 D, 2 F, 2 G, 2 I, and 1 K.

From a medium fabric, cut 1 E and 1 J.

From a medium fabric, cut 1 H.

Follow the 4" x 8" Pine Tree block cutting guide on page 136. Prepare templates A and B (pages 138–139).

From a light fabric, cut 2 A (reverse one) and 2 C.

From the theme print, cut 1 B.

From a dark fabric, cut 1 D.

From a medium fabric, cut one $4^{1}/_{2}$" x $12^{1}/_{2}$" piece for the lawn.

Block 7: Crazy Log Cabin

From the muslin, cut one 7" x 42" strip. Cut into four 7" squares.

From a dark fabric, cut four lopsided squares, about 2" across.

From the assorted fabrics, cut about 50 strips, 2" to 3" wide and 4" to 8" long.

Block 8: Fan Appliqué

Make plastic template A and freezer paper template B (pages 138–139).

From a medium fabric, cut one $12^{1}/_{2}$" square.

From the assorted fabrics, cut 7 A and 1 B.

Block 9: Sawtooth Stars

Follow the 6" block cutting guide on page 88.

From four different dark fabrics, cut 4 A.

From two dark and two light fabrics, cut 8 B each, for 32 total.

From the pink-on-cream floral print, cut 8 C and 8 D.

From two dark fabrics, cut 4 C each, for eight total, and 4 D each, for eight total.

Block 10: Roman Stripe

From a medium fabric, cut two $6^{7}/_{8}$" squares; cut diagonally in half for four triangles.

From six different fabrics, cut one $1^{1}/_{4}$" x 27" strip each.

Block 11: Nine-Patch Sampler

Prepare five freezer paper leaf templates (page 198).

From the theme print, cut the five leaf appliqués and ten $2^{1}/_{2}$" squares.

From a dark fabric, cut eight $2^{1}/_{2}$" squares.

From a light fabric, cut one $6^{1}/_{2}$" square. Cut two 4"

squares; cut diagonally in half.

From the assorted fabrics, cut nine $1^{7}/_{8}$" squares.

Block 12: Bear's Paw

This block is slightly different from the 12" block on page 118. Use either version for your sampler quilt.

From one or more dark fabrics, cut four $3^{1}/_{2}$" squares (A). Cut eight $2^{3}/_{8}$" squares; cut diagonally in half (B). Cut one $3^{1}/_{2}$" square (F).

From the pink-on-cream floral print, cut eight $2^{3}/_{8}$" squares; cut diagonally in half (C). Cut four 2" squares (D). Cut four $3^{1}/_{2}$" x 5" rectangles (E).

Block 13: Hourglass Variation

From a medium fabric, cut four $4^{1}/_{2}$" squares.

From five different contrasting fabrics, cut five $5^{1}/_{4}$" squares; cut diagonally in both directions for 20 triangles total.

Block 14: Crazy-Patch

From the muslin, cut one 13" square.

From a large print, cut one irregular triangle, 2" to 3" across, in a way that shows off the design.

From the assorted fabrics, cut 2"- to 3"-wide strips or scraps.

Block 15: Pinwheel Variation

From a dark fabric and a light fabric, cut two $2^{7}/_{8}$" x 42" strips each. Layer the strips right sides together in dark/light pairs. Cut into 18 layered $2^{7}/_{8}$" squares. Cut diagonally in half for 36 layered triangles (A, B). Do not separate the pairs; they are ready for sewing.

Block 16: Emily's Cottage

Follow the 8" Cottage block cutting guide on page 135. Prepare templates C and D (page 138).

From a medium fabric, cut 2 A, 2 C (reverse one), and 2 F.

From a dark fabric, cut 1 B.

From a dark fabric, cut 1 D.

From a dark fabric, cut 1 E, 4 G, and 2 H.

From a medium-light fabric, cut 2 I.

From a bright dark fabric, cut 1 J.

Follow the Apple Tree 4" x 8" block cutting guide on page 137.

From a medium fabric, cut 1 A, 4 C, and 2 D.

From a light fabric, cut 1 B.

From a dark fabric, cut 1 E.

From a medium fabric, cut one 4½" x 12½" piece for the lawn.

Block 17: Double Dutch

Follow the 12" block cutting guide on page 104.

From the theme print, cut 4 A and 4 C.

From a light fabric, cut 8 B, 16 D, and 4 F.

From a medium fabric, cut 4 C amd 4 E.

Block 18: Aunt Vina's Favorite

Follow the 12" block cutting guide on page 106.

From a dark fabric, cut 1 A and 8 D.

From the theme print, cut 4 B and 8 E.

From a light fabric, cut 4 C and 16 F.

Block 19: Curved Fans

Follow the 6" block cutting guide on page 154.

From the theme print, cut 4 A.

From a dark fabric, cut 4 B.

From a medium fabric, cut 4 C.

From a dark fabric, cut 8 D.

Block 20: Double Sawtooth Star

Follow the 6" block cutting guide on page 88.

From a medium fabric, cut 1 A and 8 B.

From the theme print, cut 4 C and 4 D.

Follow the 12" block cutting guide on page 88.

From the theme print, cut 8 B.

From a light fabric, cut 4 C and 4 D.

Sashing and Border

From the pink-on-cream floral print, cut twenty-four 2" x 42" strips. Set aside 17 strips for the sashing. Sew the remaining seven strips into one long strip. Cut into two 2" x 74" strips for the side borders and two 2" x 62¾" strips for the top and bottom borders.

From the brown solid, cut thirty-four ⅞" x 42" strips for the sashing accents.

From the brown theme print and another medium fabric, cut two 3⅛" x 42" strips each, or four strips total. Layer the strips right sides together in contrasting pairs. Cut into 15 layered 3⅛" squares. Cut diagonally in half for 30 layered triangles. Do not separate the pairs; they are ready for sewing.

ASSEMBLY

Refer to the Basic Block instructions to assemble blocks 1–20.

1. Make one 12" Fruit Basket block.

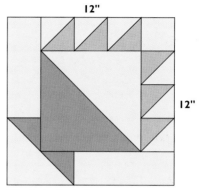

Block 1: Fruit Basket

2. Make four 6" Log Cabin blocks. Lay out the blocks to form a diagonal design as shown. Stitch the blocks together in rows. Press. Join the rows. Press.

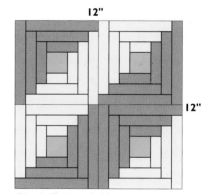

Block 2: Log Cabin

3. Make one 12" Dresden Plate block, arranging the different wedges in an ordered sequence as shown.

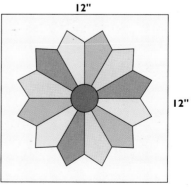

Block 3: Dresden Plate

4. Make one 12" Dolley Madison Star block.

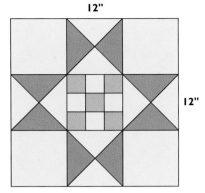

Block 4: Dolley Madison Star

5. Make 18 Flying Geese units. Arrange the units in three columns of six units each. Stitch the units together in columns. Press. Join the columns. Press.

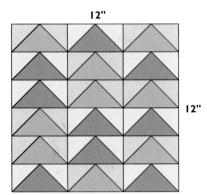

Block 5: Flying Geese

6. Make one 8" House block and one 4" x 8" Pine Tree block. Stitch together as shown. Press. Stitch the lawn piece to the bottom edge. Press.

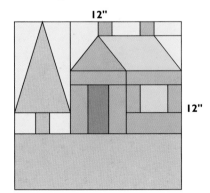

Block 6: Pinebrook

7. Make four Crazy Log Cabin blocks, using the 7" muslin squares. For this variation, called Courthouse Steps, stitch two strips to the opposite side edges of the center patch. Press. Then stitch two strips to the top and bottom edges of the center unit. Press. Continue adding strips in pairs, alternating between the sides and the top and bottom edges, until the muslin is filled. Trim each square to 6$^{1}/_{2}$" (for a 6" finished size). Stitch the squares together in rows. Press. Join the rows. Press.

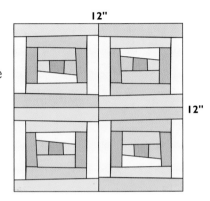

Block 7: Crazy Log Cabin

8. Refer to page 174, steps 1 and 2. Make one 12" Fan Appliqué block with seven wedges.

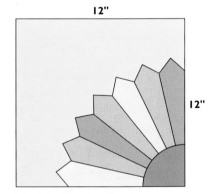

Block 8: Fan Appliqué

9. Make four 6" Sawtooth Star blocks. Lay out the blocks in a Four-Patch, alternating the light and dark backgrounds. Stitch the blocks together in rows. Press. Join the rows. Press.

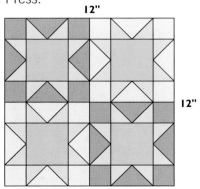

Block 9: Sawtooth Stars

10. Sew six 1¼" x 27" strips together along the long edges. Press all the seam allowances in one direction. Using the triangles as templates, cut four triangles from the striped unit (see page 72, step 2, for more details). Stitch the striped and plain triangles together in pairs to make four 6" blocks. Lay out the blocks in a Four-Patch as shown. Stitch the blocks together in rows. Press. Join the rows. Press.

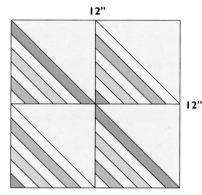

Block 10: Roman Stripe

11. Hand-appliqué five leaves to the 6½" background square. Sew eighteen 2½" squares together to make two 6" Nine-Patch blocks. Sew nine 1⅞" squares together to make a smaller Nine-Patch. Stitch a triangle to each edge for a 6" block. Lay out the blocks in a Four-Patch as shown. Stitch the blocks together in rows. Press. Join the rows. Press.

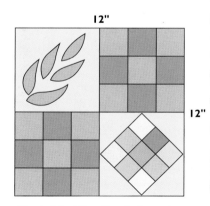

Block 11: Nine-Patch Sampler

12. Make one 12" Bear's Paw block.

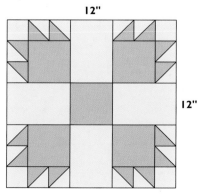

Block 12: Bear's Paw

13. Make five 4" Hourglass blocks, varying the triangle colors for each one. Arrange the Hourglass blocks and plain squares in a Nine-Patch as shown. Stitch the blocks together in rows. Press. Join the rows. Press.

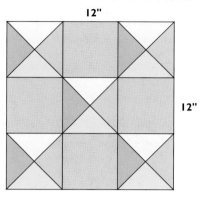

Block 13: Hourglass Variation

14. Make one Crazy-Patch block using the 13" muslin square. When the muslin is filled, trim to 12½" square (for a 12" finished size).

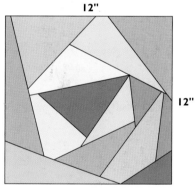

Block 14: Crazy-Patch

15. Stitch the light and dark triangles together in pairs. Join to make nine 4" Pinwheel blocks. Lay out the blocks in a Nine-Patch as shown. Stitch the blocks together in rows. Press. Join the rows. Press.

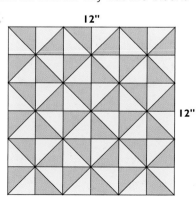

Block 15: Pinwheel Variation

16. Make one 8" Cottage block and one 4" x 8" Apple Tree block. Stitch together as shown. Press. Stitch the lawn piece to the bottom edge. Press.

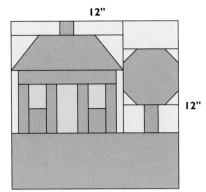

Block 16: Emily's Cottage

17. Make one 12" Double Dutch block.

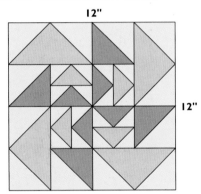

Block 17: Double Dutch

18. Make one 12" Aunt Vina's Favorite block.

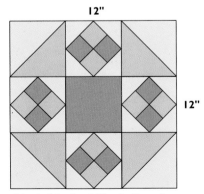

Block 18: Aunt Vina's Favorite

19. Make four 6" Curved Fan blocks. Lay out the blocks in a Four-Patch as shown. Stitch the blocks together in rows. Press. Join the rows. Press.

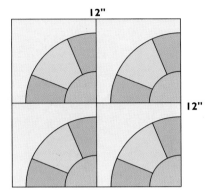

Block 19: Curved Fans

20. Make one 6" Sawtooth block. Using the 6" block as piece A, make a 12" Sawtooth block.

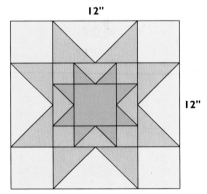

Block 20: Double Sawtooth Star

21. Sew the brown sashing accent strips to the long edges of 17 pink-on-cream sashing strips. Press toward the darker fabric. Cut into forty-nine $2^3/4$" x $12^1/2$" sashing strips. Stitch the layered triangles together as paired, and press, for 30 sashing squares.

22. Arrange the quilt blocks in five rows of four blocks each, as shown in the quilt photograph (page 190) and quilt diagram. Join the blocks together in rows, inserting sashing strips in between and at each end. Press. Stitch the remaining strips and the squares together to make six long horizontal sashing strips. Join the rows, inserting horizontal sashing strips in between and at the top and bottom. Add the side borders to the quilt top. Press. Add the top and bottom borders. Press.

23. Layer and finish the quilt. Traditional quilting lines add to the nostalgic, vintage character of *Heirloom Rose*. All the major design lines are outline-quilted. A classic diamond-and-lozenge pattern (page 198) runs through the sashing.

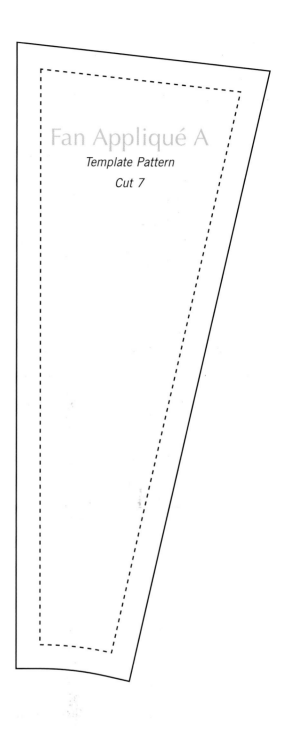

Fan Appliqué A

Template Pattern

Cut 7

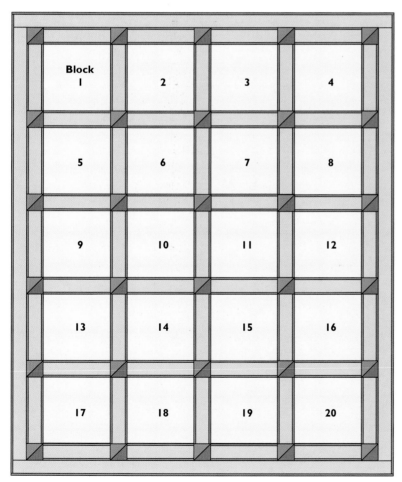

Quilt Diagram

*Heirloom Rose Leaf Appliqué
Template Patterns*

*Heirloom Rose
Diamond-and-Lozenge
Quilting Design*

Fan Appliqué

*Template Pattern B
Cut 1*

Fresh Produce

Designed by Jean Wells. Block size, 12"; quilt size, 56 1/2" x 69 1/2".

This sampler setting places four blocks on point and the remaining blocks in columns. To create interest and movement within the blocks, woven plaids in subtle colors were mixed with brighter, more intense prints. Using a dark purple plaid for the setting triangles and sashing causes the background to recede and makes the blocks more prominent. The materials list is easy to adapt to other palettes.

MATERIALS

2^1/$_2$ yards dark purple subtle plaid

Assorted orange, gold, olive green, and purple fabrics:

^{3}/$_8$ yard each 8 subtle plaids

^{1}/$_4$ yard each 10 prints

^{1}/$_8$ yard each 14 prints

^{3}/$_8$ yard for binding

3^1/$_2$ yards backing

^{3}/$_8$ yard muslin

61" x 74" batting

CUTTING

Cut the pieces for each block, using the assorted plaids and prints and, occasionally, the dark purple subtle plaid. Refer to the quilt photograph (page 199) for ideas on how to combine different colors and fabric designs.

Block 1: Log Cabin

Follow the 6" block cutting guide on page 53.

From a print, cut 4 A.

From the assorted greens, cut 2 B, 2 C, 2 F, 2 G, 2 J, and 2 K.

From the assorted golds, cut 2 B, 2 C, 2 F, 2 G, 2 J, and 2 K.

From the assorted purples, cut 2 D, 2 E, 2 H, 2 I, 2 L, and 2 M.

From the assorted oranges, cut 2 D, 2 E, 2 H, 2 I, 2 L, and 2 M.

Block 2: Aunt Vina's Favorite

Follow the 12" block cutting guide on page 106.

From a purple print, cut 1 A and 4 B.

From a gold plaid, cut 4 C, 8 E, and 16 F.

From a green print, cut 8 D.

Block 3: Curved Fans

Follow the 6" block cutting guide on page 154.

Choose three fabrics for each fan, or four sets total. From each set, cut 1 D, 1 E, and 2 F.

From an orange plaid, cut 4 B.

Block 4: Pinebrook

Follow the 8" House block cutting guide on page 134. Prepare templates C, D, and E (pages 138–139).

From a gold plaid, cut 3 A and 2 C (reverse one).

From an orange plaid, cut 2 B.

From a purple print, cut 1 D, 2 F, 2 G, 2 I, and 1 K.

From an orange print, cut 1 E.

From a green print, cut 1 H.

From a bright orange print, cut 1 J.

Follow the 4" x 8" Pine Tree block cutting guide on page 136. Prepare templates A and B (pages 138–139).

From a gold plaid, cut 2 A (reverse one) and 2 C.

From a green print, cut 1 B.

From a dark orange print, cut 1 D.

From a green/orange print, cut one 4^1/$_2$" x 12^1/$_2$" piece for the lawn.

Block 5: Double Dutch

Follow the 12" block cutting guide on page 104.

From a gold print, cut 4 A.

From a green plaid, cut 8 B, 16 D, and 4 F.

From an orange print, cut 4 C.

From a purple print, cut 4 C and 4 E.

Block 6: Pinwheel Variation

From a plaid and a multicolor print, cut one 2⅞" x 42" strip each. Layer the strips right sides together. Cut into six layered 2⅞" squares; cut diagonally in half for 12 layered triangles. Do not separate the pairs; they are ready for sewing. Repeat twice more, using a different plaid each time, for 36 paired triangles total.

Block 7: Emily's Cottage

Follow the 8" Cottage block cutting guide on page 135. Prepare templates C and D (page 138).

From an orange plaid, cut 2 A, 2 C (reverse one), and 2 F.

From a purple plaid, cut 1 B, 1 E, 4 G, and 2 H.

From a green print, cut 1 D.

From a gold print, cut 2 I.

From a bright orange print, cut 1 J.

Follow the 4" x 8" Apple Tree block cutting guide on page 137.

From an orange plaid, cut 1 A, 4 C, and 2 D.

From a multicolor floral print, cut 1 B.

From a dark olive print, cut 1 E.

From a green plaid, cut one 4½" x 12½" piece for the lawn.

Block 8: Crazy-Patch

From the muslin, cut one 13" square.

From a large print, cut one irregular triangle, 2" to 3" across, in a way that shows off the design.

From the assorted fabrics, cut 2"- to 3"-wide strips or scraps.

Block 9: Nine-Patch Variation

Follow the 6" block cutting guide on page 105.

From a gold plaid and a green plaid, cut two 4" squares each; cut diagonally in half for eight setting triangles.

From the assorted fabrics, cut thirty-six 1⅞" squares.

Block 10: Dolley Madison Star

Follow the 12" block cutting guide on page 86.

From a purple print, cut 5 A and 8 C.

From a green print, cut 4 B.

From a light orange print, cut 4 D.

From a gold plaid, cut 4 D and 4 E.

Block 11: Bear's Paw

Follow the 12" block cutting guide on page 118.

From a multicolor print, cut 4 A and 1 F.

From a purple print, cut 16 B.

From an orange plaid, cut 16 C, 4 D, and 4 E.

Block 12: Fruit Basket

Follow the 12" block cutting guide on page 119.

From a green print, cut 1 A.

From a gold plaid, cut 1 B, 6 D, 1 E, 2 F, and 1 H.

From an orange print, cut 2 G.

From a purple print, cut 6 C.

Block 13: Dresden Plate

Follow the 12" block cutting guide on page 168. Prepare plastic template A and freezer paper template B (page 172).

From a green plaid, cut one 12½" square.

From the assorted prints, cut 12 A and 1 B.

Block 14: Double Sawtooth Star

Follow the 6" block cutting guide on page 88.

From an orange print, cut 1 A and 8 B.

From a green print, cut 4 C and 4 D.

Follow the 12" block cutting guide on page 88.

From a green print, cut 8 B.

From an orange plaid, cut 4 C and 4 D.

Flying Geese Strips

From the orange, green, and gold prints, cut a total of four 2" x 42" strips. Cut into forty-eight 2" x 3½" rectangles.

From the purple plaid, cut five 2" x 42" strips. Cut into ninety-six 2" squares. Cut two 3½" x 42" strips. Cut into the following pieces: one 3" x 3½" (A), two 3½" squares (B), one 4" x 3½" (C), one 5½" x 3½" (D), three 6" x 3½" (E), one 6½" x 3½" (F), three 7" x 3½" (G), and one 7½" x 3½" (H).

Setting Triangles

From the purple plaid, cut two 18⅜" squares. Cut diagonally in both directions for six setting triangles (two are discarded). Cut two 9¾" squares. Cut diagonally in half for four corner setting triangles.

Sashing and Border

From the purple plaid, cut fifteen 2" x 42" strips. Cut into twelve 2" x 12$\frac{1}{2}$" strips for the horizontal sashing/borders. Sew the remaining strips into one long strip. Cut into six 2" x 69$\frac{1}{2}$" strips for the vertical sashing/borders.

ASSEMBLY

1. Make two green/purple 6" Log Cabin blocks. Make two orange/gold 6" Log Cabin blocks. Lay out the blocks in a Four-Patch as shown to form a diamond design. Stitch the blocks together in rows. Press. Join the rows. Press.

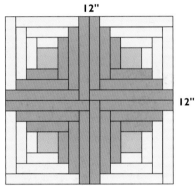

Block 1: Log Cabin

2. Make one 12" Aunt Vina's Favorite block.

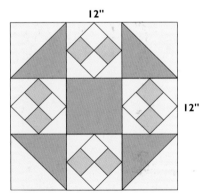

Block 2: Aunt Vina's Favorite

3. Make four 6" Curved Fan blocks. Lay out the blocks in a Four-Patch as shown. Stitch the blocks together in rows. Press. Join the rows. Press.

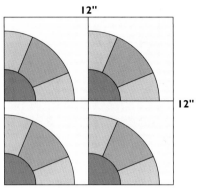

Block 3: Curved Fans

4. Make one 8" House block and one 4" x 8" Pine Tree block. Stitch together as shown. Press. Stitch the lawn piece to the bottom edge. Press.

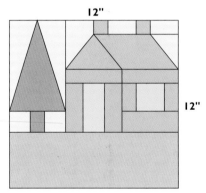

Block 4: Pinebrook

5. Make one 12" Double Dutch block.

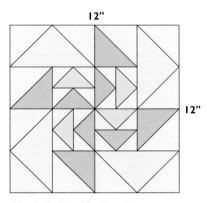

Block 5: Double Dutch

6. Stitch the plaid and print triangles together in pairs. Join to make three 4" Pinwheel blocks for each color plaid, or nine total. Lay out the blocks in a Nine-Patch as shown. Stitch the blocks together in rows. Press. Join the rows. Press.

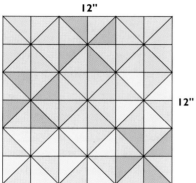

Block 6: Pinwheel Variation

7. Make one 8" Cottage block and one 4" x 8" Apple Tree block. Stitch together as shown. Press. Stitch the lawn piece to the bottom edge. Press.

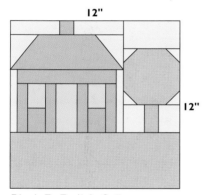

Block 7: Emily's Cottage

8. Make one Crazy-Patch block using the 13" muslin square. When the muslin is filled, trim to $12^{1}/_{2}$" square (for a 12" finished size).

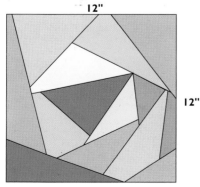

Block 8: Crazy-Patch

9. Make four 6" Nine-Patch-in-a-Square blocks, two with gold plaid triangles and two with green plaid triangles. Lay out the blocks in a Four-Patch as shown. Stitch the blocks together in rows. Press. Join the rows. Press.

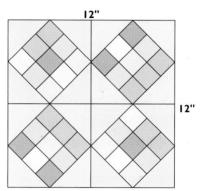

Block 9: Nine-Patch Variation

10. Make one 12" Dolley Madison Star block. Orient the CD units so that the light orange triangles form a ring around the Nine-Patch.

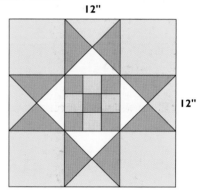

Block 10: Dolley Madison Star

11. Make one 12" Bear's Paw block.

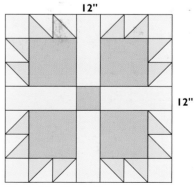

Block 11: Bear's Paw

12. Make one 12" Fruit Basket block.

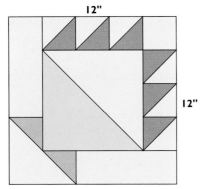

Block 12: Fruit Basket

13. Make one 12" Dresden Plate block.

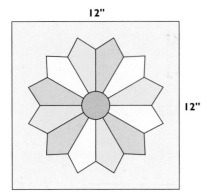

Block 13: Dresden Plate

14. Make one 6" Sawtooth Star block. Using the 6" block as piece A, make a 12" Sawtooth Star block.

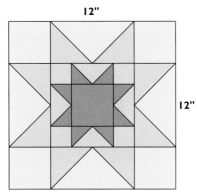

Block 14: Double Sawtooth Star

15. Use the 2" purple squares and the 2" x 3¹/₂" assorted rectangles to make 48 Flying Geese units. Stitch the units together, choosing the colors at random and pressing as you go, to make the following: 3 two-geese units, 3 three-geese units, 1 four-geese unit, 3 five-geese units, and 2 seven-geese units. Lay out the units and pieces A through H in two columns, as shown in the quilt diagram. Stitch the pieces together, pressing toward the solid pieces after each addition.

Flying Geese
Make 48 assorted

16. Lay out the blocks, setting triangles, and Flying Geese columns, as shown in the quilt photograph (page 199) and quilt diagram. Join blocks 1–10 in two columns, inserting horizontal sashing strips in between and at each end. Press toward the sashing. Stitch blocks 11–14 and the setting triangles in diagonal rows. Press toward the setting triangles. Join the diagonal rows. Press. Add the corner triangles. Press. Join all the columns, inserting vertical sashing strips in between and at each side edge.

17. Layer and finish the quilt. Outline-quilt the basic blocks and shapes to stabilize the quilt sandwich, and then get creative. Seed catalogs offer lots of images for quilting the setting triangles. Peapods, cabbages, eggplant, corn, carrots, radishes, tomatoes, and flowers are some of the images quilter Patricia Raymond enlarged on a photocopier to fit these open spaces. They contribute so much to the "fresh produce" theme.

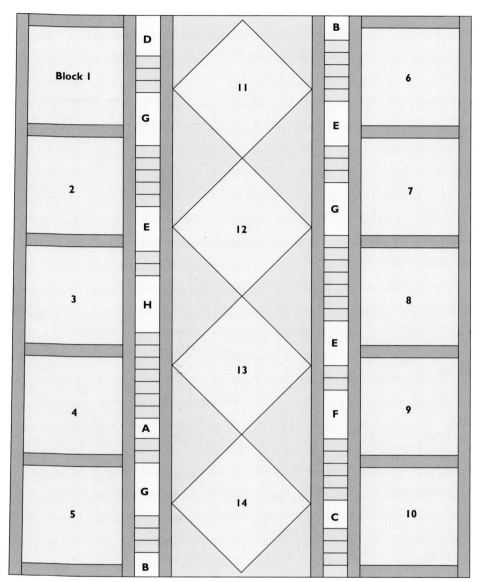

Quilt Diagram

Sources

The Stitchin' Post
P.O. Box 280
311 West Cascade
Sisters, OR 97759
(541) 549-6061
stitchin@stitchinpost.com
www.stitchinpost.com
The Stitchin' Post stocks over 7500 bolts of fabric—batiks, florals, reproduction prints, whimsical cottons—plus quilting books, rotary cutters, template plastic, fusible appliqué supplies, and almost anything else a quilter would want. Call or write for a mail order catalog or visit the website.

Cotton Patch Mail Order
3405 Hall Lane, Dept. CTB
Lafayette, CA 94595
(800) 835-4418
quiltusa@yahoo.com
www.quiltusa.com
A complete quilting supply store.

More favorites by C&T Publishing:

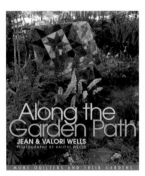

Along the Garden Path
More Quilters and Their Gardens
by Jean & Valori Wells

Garden-Inspired Quilts
Design Journals for 12 Quilt Projects
by Jean & Valori Wells

Four Seasons in Flannel
23 Projects—Quilts & More
by Jean Wells & Lawry Thorn

Radiant New York Beauties
14 Paper-Pieced Quilt Projects
by Valori Wells

Everything Flowers
Quilts from the Garden
by Jean & Valori Wells

Through the Garden Gate
Quilts from the Garden
by Jean & Valori Wells

Stitch 'n Flip Quilts
14 Fantastic Projects
by Valori Wells

About the Author

Jean Wells has been an avid quilter for over thirty years, sharing her knowledge and ideas with thousands of quilters of all experience levels. A teacher at heart, she began sewing as a child, and her love of sewing led to a career as a home economics teacher and school counselor. Twenty-seven years ago, she opened her quilt shop, The Stitchin' Post, in Sisters, Oregon, a small 1880s-style town at the foot of the Cascade mountains. The Stitchin' Post is one of the very first quilt shops to be opened in America and today is one of the premier shops featured in *American Patchwork & Quilting* magazine's "Quilt Shop Sampler."

Jean has written articles for magazines, lectured and taught quilting classes worldwide, conducted business classes for fellow quilt shop owners, and appeared on numerous television shows, including HGTV's *Simply Quilts*. A recipient of the Michael Kile Award for lifetime achievement in the quilting industry, Jean was inducted into the Primedia Hall of Fame as one of the first "independent retailers" and also received her local community's "Business of the Year" award.

A love of gardening led Jean to open her second retail store, The Wild Hare, also in Sisters, where she offers unique garden-style accessories and decorative items. The combination of quilting and gardening has proved especially fruitful for Jean, and she often explores garden-related themes in her quiltmaking. In 2000, her quilt *Paradise in the Garden* won the Millennium Quilt Contest's Imagination Award. She used the cash prize to build a small greenhouse garden shed, which she has surrounded with flowers and vegetables.

Index